PSYCHOANALYTIC LISTENING

PSYCHOANALYTIC LISTENING

Methods, Limits, and Innovations

Salman Akhtar

KARNAC

First published in 2013 by
Karnac Books Ltd
118 Finchley Road
London NW3 5HT

British Library Cataloguing in Publication Data

A C.I.P. for this book is available from the British Library

ISBN-13: 978-1-78049-145-5

Typeset by V Publishing Solutions (P) Ltd., Chennai, India

www.karnacbooks.com

To

OTTO KERNBERG

With admiration, affection, and gratitude

"We can imagine a mute analyst, but not a deaf one"

—*Leopold Nosek*, 2009

CONTENTS

ACKNOWLEDGEMENTS

Dr Michael Vergare, chairman of the Department of Psychiatry and Human Behavior at the Jefferson Medical College (my academic base for over thirty years), has consistently supported my work. My patients mobilised the sort of technical questions that this book attempts to answer. Drs Jennifer Bonovitz, Ira Brenner, Axel Hoffer, Judith Kark, Joshua Levy, and Vamik Volkan provided information that was useful for this book. My wife and fellow analyst, Monisha Akhtar, gave useful input and sustained the ambience necessary for creative work. Chapter Two of this book was specifically written on the behest of Dr Teresa Lorito of Pisa, Italy, and benefitted from the input of Drs Daniela Bolelli, Stefano Calamandrei, Giovanni Foresti, Paula Freer, and Maria Grazia Vassallo during its presentation at the Silenzo Umano, Silenzo Disumano Conference in Pisa in June, 2011. My assistant, Jan Wright, prepared the manuscript of the book with her characteristic diligence and good humour. To all these individuals, my sincere thanks indeed.

ABOUT THE AUTHOR

Salman Akhtar, MD, is professor of psychiatry at Jefferson Medical College and a training and supervising analyst at the Psychoanalytic Center of Philadelphia. He has served on the editorial boards of the *International Journal of Psychoanalysis* and the *Journal of the American Psychoanalytic Association*. His more than 300 publications include thirteen books—*Broken Structures* (1992), *Quest for Answers* (1995), *Inner Torment* (1999), *Immigration and Identity* (1999), *New Clinical Realms* (2003), *Objects of Our Desire* (2005), *Regarding Others* (2007), *Turning Points in Dynamic Psychotherapy* (2009), *The Damaged Core* (2009), *Comprehensive Dictionary of Psychoanalysis* (2009), *Immigration and Acculturation* (2011), *Matters of Life and Death* (2011), and *The Book of Emotions* (2012)—as well as forty-one edited or co-edited volumes in psychiatry and psychoanalysis. Dr Akhtar has delivered many prestigious addresses and lectures including, most recently, the inaugural address at the first IPA-Asia Congress in Beijing, China (2010). Dr Akhtar is the recipient of the *Journal of the American Psychoanalytic Association's* Best Paper of the Year Award (1995), the Margaret Mahler Literature Prize (1996), the American Society of Psychoanalytic Physicians' Sigmund Freud Award (2000), the American College of Psychoanalysts' Laughlin Award (2003), the American Psychoanalytic Association's Edith

Sabshin Award (2000), Columbia University's Robert Liebert Award for Distinguished Contributions to Applied Psychoanalysis (2004), the American Psychiatric Association's Kun Po Soo Award (2004), Irma Bland Award for being the Outstanding Teacher of Psychiatric Residents (2005), and Nancy Roeske Award for being the Outstanding Teacher of Medical Students (2012). Dr Akhtar is an internationally sought speaker and teacher, and his books have been translated into many languages, including German, Turkish, and Romanian. His interests are wide and he has served as the film review editor for the *International Journal of Psychoanalysis*, and is currently serving as the book review editor for the *International Journal of Applied Psychoanalytic Studies*, and an editorial reader for the *Psychoanalytic Quarterly*. He has published seven collections of poetry and serves as a scholar-in-residence at the InterAct Theatre Company in Philadelphia.

INTRODUCTION

Joseph Breuer's celebrated patient, Anna O., designated psychoanalysis to be a "talking cure". She was correct insofar as psychoanalysis does place verbal exchange at centre stage. Indeed, the "fundamental rule" of analytic technique is that the patient must say what comes to mind. He or she must not avoid talking about something on syntactical, aesthetic, and moral grounds. The counterpart to such "free association" on the patient's part was the analyst's spoken words. These "interventions" were varied and, with the maturation of psychoanalysis as a clinical discipline, a great variety of them gradually evolved. The concept of "interpretation" alone was broken down into the subcategories of transference interpretation, extra-transference interpretation, genetic interpretation, inexact interpretation, deep interpretation, anagogic interpretation, and so on. As if this were not enough, further types of interventions evolved including clarification, construction, reconstruction, bridging intervention, affirmative intervention, depth-rendering intervention, developmental intervention, and the like.

The focus upon the patient's and therapist's *speaking* activities diverted attention from how the two parties *listen* to each other. The following questions thus got ignored. Is analytic listening different from ordinary listening? What are the prerequisites for analytic listening? Is only one type of listening required during analytic sessions? If there is more than one type of listening required, then what determines the use of one particular type at a given moment? How does one or the other variety of listening affect one's interventions? What is one listening for? Does one listen to words, gaps between words, or the music of affect that pervades the analytic session? Can one "listen" to silences, visual images, postural changes, and other non-verbal communications? Should the analyst's listening be restricted to what the patient says or does or can it be directed at the analyst's own mind and behaviour? And so on and so forth.

One can add some patient-focused questions on the topic as well. Does the patient actually listen when the analyst speaks? Does the patient listen to the analyst's words or his or her tone of voice? How does the patient listen to himself or herself? Are the patients' listening skills characterological in origin, or can they be enhanced by analysis itself? To be sure, this list, too, can be readily expanded. The point is this: what Anna O. said was true but it hardly constituted the whole truth. Psychoanalysis is a listening *and* talking cure. Both elements are integral to clinical work. Listening with no talking can only go so far. Talking without listening can mislead and harm. And yet, the listening end of the equation has received short shrift in analytic literature.

My book aims to rectify this problem by focusing upon analytic listening. Taking Freud's early description of how an analyst ought to listen as its starting point, the book traverses considerable historical, theoretical, and clinical territory. The ground covered ranges from diverse methods of listening through the informative potential of the countertransference to the outer limits of our customary attitude where psychoanalytic listening no longer helps and might even be contraindicated. Allow me, at this point, to briefly comment upon each of these chapters.

In the opening chapter of the book, I describe four models of analytic listening: (i) objective listening, (ii) subjective listening, (iii) empathic listening, and (iv) intersubjective listening. Each has its theoretical anchors and its technical yields. After elucidating these, I unmask the areas of overlap in the aforementioned models and also note some hybrid forms that have fallen between partisan cracks. I trace the developmental roots of various forms of listening and link the emergent polarity in this realm (i.e., credulous vs. sceptical) with the maternal and paternal forms of relating to children. I suggest that an optimal blend of the two poles makes analytic listening better attuned (and useful) to the patient. Needless to add, such listening is directed to the patient's words as well as to his non-verbal communications.

Picking up this last-mentioned theme, I address the multifaceted phenomenon of silence in the next chapter. In it, I outline eight types of silence: (i) structural silence, (ii) silence due to the lack of mentalisation, (iii) silence due to conflict, (iv) silence as enactment, (v) symbolic silence, (vi) contemplative silence, (vii) regenerative silence, and (viii) blank silence. I place silence on an equal footing with speaking by emphasising that both have the ability to serve similar aims. Both can hide and both can express psychic contents. Both can defend against drive-related pressures and both can help discharge such tensions. Both can convey transference and both can become vehicles of enactment. Both can induce and evoke countertransference feelings. Both can facilitate or impede the progress of the analytic process. Through all this and more, both silence and verbalisation become integral to our clinical enterprise. However, the aims and consequences of the patient's silence and the analyst's silence might differ. In addition to delineating the technical principles involving their concurrent silences, I describe the phenomenon of "mutual silence" in the clinical hour and elucidate its ontogenetic as well as anagogic foundations.

The discussion of silence leads me to the next logical stopping point, that is, all that is communicated by the patient in the form of action. This forms the topic of the next chapter of this book. I divide my discourse into listening to actions (i) while arranging the first visit, (ii) as the patient arrives for the first visit, (iii) during this initial consultation, (iv) during the beginning phase of analysis, (v) during the middle phase of analysis, and (vi) during the termination phase of analysis. Considering them as messages about his psychopathological state and—later, in the course of the treatment—about his transference relatedness, I tackle the thorny issue of interpreting these behavioural aspects during our clinical work.

In the chapter that follows, I shift my attention from listening to the patient's material to the sort of information the psychoanalyst can draw from "listening" to his own self. I review the broad and evolving concept of countertransference, under the rubric of which the experiences I describe tend to belong. With admittedly undue precision, I categorise the psychoanalyst's informative self-vigilance into (i) listening to one's associations, (ii) listening to one's emotions, (iii) listening to one's impulses, and (iv) listening to one's actions. I demonstrate that the analyst's paying attention to his subjective experience is a rich source of information about the nature of his analysand's communications as well as the silently unfolding events in the transference-countertransference axis. Awareness of how one's subjective experience can be "inspected" from various perspectives is especially helpful to the analyst during emotionally turbulent moments of clinical work. I extend this idea in useful directions by utilising a synthesis of the ego-psychological, object relations, and the *au courant* relational and intersubjective vantage points. The same conceptual scaffold deepens our understanding of how our capacity for analytic listening gets seriously compromised.

This constitutes the topic of my next chapter. In it, I delineate six variables that have the potential of impeding psychoanalytic listening: (i) hearing impairment, (ii) characterological resistance on the analyst's part, (iii) countertransference blocks, (iv) conceptual rigidity and an unshakeable commitment to this or that theoretical model, (v) marked sociocultural difference between the analyst and the patient, and (vi) bilingualism of one or both parties in the therapeutic dyad. Many of these variables can exist simultaneously and one variable (e.g., conceptual rigidity) can be affected by another (e.g., countertransference blocks). Some factors (e.g., mild hearing loss) might be remediable while others (e.g., cultural difference) are there to stay. One must nonetheless be aware of their potentially deleterious impact upon analytic listening. I attempt to make such impact vivid and convincing by bringing forth corroborative evidence from earlier literature and by offering suggestive clinical vignettes from my practice.

In the next chapter, I note that speech itself can serve as a resistance to the analytic process. I then raise the tricky question of whether listening is always "good" and helpful. I suggest that the analyst might actually refuse to listen: (i) when the patient is attempting to pull the analyst into a misalliance from the very outset, (ii) when the patient is repeating something *ad nauseum*, (iii) when the patient is using speech for instinctual discharge or narcissistic stabilisation, and (iv) when the patient is bringing forth a much-analysed transference in an unconsciously playful manner towards the end of the analysis. However, refusal to listen is a technical strategy that (i) should be utilised only by those with considerable clinical experience, (ii) should be used sparingly, (iii) should be used after much affirmative and interpretive work has been done, (iv) should be made after consultation with a colleague, and, if that is not possible, its use must be discussed post-hoc with a colleague, (v) should be used after an earnest effort has been made to disentangle countertransference temptations from genuine therapeutic intent, and (vi) requires that its impact upon the patient be looked for and analytically handled. Also to be underscored is that even when the analyst refuses to listen, the analyst actually does not stop listening. What he does is stop listening to surface material and start insisting that the patient go deeper.

Having elucidated all these aspects of analytic listening, I attempt to demonstrate the restrictions we must put on this prized capacity of ours. In the final chapter of the book, I describe how psychoanalytic listening needs to be tempered in the following three situations: (i) during supervision, (ii) in public discourse, and (iii) at home. In supervision, we should restrict our analytic listening to the control patient's material and to the patient-candidate relationship, eliminating speculation about the candidate's internal object and his or her overall character. In public discourse, we must temper the risk of becoming a "wild analyst" and remind ourselves of the inappropriateness of the setting and the lack of supportive data. In domestic life, we should try to put analytic listening aside as much as possible and not let technical jargon crowd out the vernacular of "ordinary" human conversation. Such restraints on the use of our analytic minds paradoxically sharpen their edge.

The brief glimpse I have offered here into the contents of the book's seven chapters does not do justice to them. Their layering of history, their coverage of literature, their anchor in theory, their provision of clinical vignettes, and their intricate relationships with each other yield a multifaceted and nuanced discourse on the topic of analytic listening. It is my sincere hope that such effort and integrative striving would help prospective and novice analysts in fine-tuning their listening capacities. If those who are truly experienced in our field, too, find something of meaning here, I would be happier.

CHAPTER ONE

Four kinds of analytic listening

"[The analyst] must turn his own unconscious like a receptive organ towards the transmitting unconscious of the patient"

—Sigmund Freud (1912e, p. 115)

In his papers on psychoanalytic technique, Freud (1911e, 1912b, 1912e, 1913c, 1914g, 1915a) dealt with almost all important aspects of our clinical enterprise, including the need for a certain frequency and regularity of sessions, payment, use of the couch, free association, the limits of memory and recall, resistance, transference, anonymity and neutrality, working with dreams, and interpretive interventions of the analyst. He also made a number of remarks about the analyst's manner of listening and what exactly it is that he ought to be attuned towards in his attention. Note the following recommendations made by Freud in this context.

- "The technique … is a very simple one … It consists simply in not directing one's notice to anything in particular and in maintaining the same 'evenly suspended attention' in the face of all that one hears" (1912e, pp. 111–112).

- "The rule for the doctor may be expressed: 'He should withhold all conscious influences from his capacity to attend, and give himself over completely to his "unconscious memory".' Or, to put it in terms of technique: 'He should simply listen and not bother about whether he is keeping anything in mind'" (ibid., p. 112).
- "He must turn over his own unconscious like a receptive organ towards the transmitting unconscious of the patient. He must adjust himself to the patient as a telephone receiver is adjusted to the transmitting microphone … the doctor's unconscious is able, from the derivatives of the unconscious which are communicated to him, to reconstruct that unconscious which has determined the patient's free associations" (ibid., pp. 115–116).

It is clear that Freud put immense trust in the direct communication between the patient's and the analyst's unconscious and held the analyst's free-floating attention to be the outer half of the patient's free association. This is not to say that Freud was not cognizant of the hindrance to the treatment caused by unresolved problems in the analyst's personality. He exhorted the prospective analyst to "not tolerate any resistances in himself" (ibid., p. 116), undergo an analysis himself, and "continue the analytic examination of his personality in the form of a self-analysis" (ibid., p. 117). Otherwise, there was a risk of not listening to the patient properly, omitting cues offered by the patient and, worse, projecting one's own personal issues on the matters under consideration.

Analytic listening, for Freud, was not restricted to the patient's spoken words. It also included paying attention to his silences, and to the non-verbal cues he offered (Freud, 1909d, 1914g, 1917). Attention of such breadth required a relaxed submission to all the input that was coming one's way. There was no scope for focusing, choosing, or censoring here. In a later paper, Freud reiterated that

> We gather the material for our work from a variety of sources— from what is conveyed to us by the information given us by the patient and by his free associations, from what he shows us in his transferences, from what we arrive at by interpreting his dreams, and from what he betrays by his slips or parapraxes. All this material helps us to make constructions about what happened to him and has been forgotten as well as what is happening in him now without his understanding it. (1940a, pp. 177–178)

For such a transaction to take place, the analyst had to make sure that he was not putting up resistances in the pathway to listening; the best way to assure this was to undergo a "psychoanalytic purification" (Freud, 1912e, p. 116) himself. This was especially important for handling transference love with equanimity since an analyst who has worked-through his narcissism would understand that "the patient's falling in love is induced by the analytic situation and is not to be attributed to the charms of his own person" (Freud, 1915a, p. 161). However, arriving at such a mental posture, especially on the novice's part, required some effort.[1] The tension between the passive surrender to an "evenly hovering" state of mind and the active measures undertaken to enter that state of mind is something that later contributors have had to struggle with. They also had to face the paradox that the analyst's not listening to anything in particular is precisely what leads one to find things that are particularly significant. Psychoanalytic contributors who came after Freud thus found their own solutions to these dilemmas and added further nuances to the manner in which an analyst listens to the patient's communication.[2]

Given the broad spectrum of these listening styles and the great diversity of what their respective proponents focus upon, any attempt at categorising them is bound to falter or remain incomplete. Moreover, the various ways of listening that have evolved are not surgically apart; they show significant overlaps. With such caveats in mind, I propose that in the literature subsequent to Freud's (1912e) original ideas about the topic, psychoanalytic listening has been described in four major ways. These include (i) objective listening, (ii) subjective listening, (iii) empathic listening, and (iv) intersubjective listening. Each perspective deserves separate consideration though without overlooking its complementarity and confluence with its counterparts.

Objective listening

This manner of listening has its foundations in the "classic" vision of human nature, its maladies and their amelioration. Such a perspective, found most clearly in Kant's thought, holds striving towards autonomy and reign of reason to be the essence of being human. Extrapolated to psychoanalysis,

> The classic view sees man as governed by the pleasure principle and the development towards maturity is that towards the

predominance of the reality principle. The analyst's attitude towards the patient is a combination of respect and suspicion and the analyst takes the side of the reality principle. The ethic is stoic: maturity and mental health depend on the extent to which a person can acknowledge reality as it is and be rational and wise. (Strenger, 1989, p. 601)

The "classic" attitude places the analyst in the position of detached observer and an arbiter of "reality" and, when it comes to analytic listening, prompts a certain amount of scepticism regarding the patient's verbal productions. The analyst's listening does not get seduced by the patient's avowed difficulties. It is propelled towards deciphering "the ways in which the patient's wishes and fantasies colour his perception of reality, past and present" (ibid., p. 603). Attention is paid to *what* the patient is talking about but greater interest remains in *how* the patient is talking; the process is accorded more value than the content. Consequently, pauses, hesitations, emphases, peculiarities of intonation, and slips of the tongue evoke the analyst's interest to a greater extent than the "story" on the patient's mind.

This perspective on analytic listening ardently upholds the value of the patient's "free association". Its proponents (Brenner, 1976; Busch, 1997, 2004; Fenichel, 1941; Gray, 1994; Hoffer, 2006; Kris, 1982, 1992) assert that it is only by following the patient's chain of thoughts—and impediments to it—that one can gain access to the unconscious meanings of the patient's conflicts. To be sure, over the course of time, the purview of what falls under the rubric of "free association" has enlarged (see Peter Fonagy's remarks in McDermott, 2003) to include visual images (Kanzer, 1958; Warren, 1961), bodily movements and postural changes on the couch (McLaughlin, 1987, 1992), and even an occasional invitation for the patient to draw something that he or she is finding difficult to put into words (Brakel, 1993; Slap, 1976). Also pertinent in this context is Makari and Shapiro's (1993) clarification that analytic listening attends to non-linguistic communications as well as the subtle linguistic categories pertaining to narrativity, symbolic reference, form, idiom, and interaction convention. An unmistakable feature of an analyst listening "objectively" is that he relies less on his intuition and more on his intellectual capacity, however "silently" the latter might operate during his clinical work. Brenner's (1976) painstakingly methodical way to arrive at a "conjecture" or "an analyst's formulation in his own mind of what he has learned about the patient's conflicts" (p. 36) exemplifies such a stance. Without ruling out the element of sudden subjective grasp of meanings inherent in the patient's communication, Brenner puts a premium upon the step-by-step, logical, and intellectual process of conjecture formation. In no uncertain terms, he states that it is "important to keep in mind one's analytic knowledge of symptom formation and to apply it when one is analyzing patients" (p. 21), and that "whatever the patient reports or does should be viewed in the same way, i.e., in the light of the analyst's understanding of the nature, the origin, and the consequences of conflict in psychic life" (p. 29).[3] To this end, Brenner (2000)—later in his analytic career—went so far as to suggest that a selective and strategical shifting of focus of attention is more useful than "evenly suspended attention" (Freud, 1912e, p. 111) in listening to analytic material.

More sustained respect for the data obtained from listening to the patient's free association was demonstrated by Gray (1982, 1994). His suggested method of listening hones in on the moment-to-moment shifts of direction, emphasis, and nuance in the stream of the patient's associations. It pays sharp attention to a pause, an abrupt change of topic, the emergence of an incongruent affect, and an unexplained avoidance of the logically expectable. Such "close process monitoring" (Gray, 1982) places the ego in the centre of psychodynamic technique, helps unmask transference proclivities, and facilitates resistance analysis. Busch (1997, 2004) has further elaborated upon this manner of working with patients.

The Kleinians, though opposed to such "ego psychology" in important theoretical ways, demonstrate equal interest in the moment-to-moment changes in the flow and direction of the patient's thought. However, they tend to regard all free associations as referring to transference (Hinshelwood, 1989; Klein, 1952; Riviere, 1952). Moreover, unlike the ego psychologists who focus upon *what causes the turn* in the flow of the patient's associations, the Kleinians are interested in *what is caused by the turn* in the flow of the patient's associations. This is because the Kleinians regard free associations themselves as actions.[4]

Subjective listening

Standing apart from the analysts who listen "objectively" are those who rely a great deal upon their subjectivity in their attempts to understand what the patient is trying to communicate. To such analysts, understanding often comes in the form of inspiration with no (or very little) conscious effort to put the "two plus two" of the situation together. They subscribe to Freud's (1912e) declaration that the analyst's unconscious, if properly attuned, is directly able to pick up what the patient's unconscious is transmitting. Reik's (1937) warning that conscious logical thinking is detrimental to analytic perception advances this line of thinking. Isaacs's (1939) statement that a conjecture about the patient's intent is of the nature of a perception also embodies the spirit of an intuitive way of functioning during the clinical hour. Yet another illustration is formed by Bion's (1967) grim declaration that since "memory is always misleading … [and] desires distort judgment" (p. 271), it is best that the analyst should listen to the patient without memory or desire. It is only then that the ultimate truth of the moment—"O" in Bion's (1965, 1967) terminology—will become evident. The sudden and sharp clarity would then lead to the "act of faith" (Bion, 1970), that is, an analytic intervention that is based upon intuition and has left experience and knowledge behind.

Less dramatic and far more systematically presented are the views of Jacobs (1973, 1986, 1991, 2007). He holds firmly to the analyst's counterpart for the "fundamental rule" (Freud, 1913c, p. 134) for the patient: the injunction that the analyst should privately consider all that occurs within him for its potentially informative value in terms of the patient and in terms of what is taking place between the two of them. More than any other analyst—perhaps with the exception of Searles (1979), who largely dealt with severely ill and often psychotic patients—Jacobs relies upon his inner emotional state, his passing associations, his reverie, and even his attire and postural changes to discern the events that are taking place between him and his patient but are just so slightly out of the conscious awareness of both. He notes that:

> The manner in which the analyst begins and ends a session; his posture, facial expressions and tone as he greets or says goodbye to his patient, convey kinesic messages of which he may or may not be himself be cognizant …. There is, however, another aspect of the analyst's non-verbal behavior that has received relatively little emphasis in the literature: the bodily movements that accompany the act of listening. Certain of these movements, such as tapping a foot or motor restlessness may, through sound, be conveyed to the

patient, and, in fact, act as conscious and unconscious communications. At other times, the patient may detect from the slightest
acoustical clues an otherwise unexpressed attitude or feeling on the
part of the analyst. (1991, p. 104)

Jacobs goes on to speak of "body empathy", or the increased cathexis
of the body ego that accompanies well-attuned listening. The analyst's
bodily responses reverberate with the patient's unconscious communication. By paying attention to his own posture, gestures, and movement, the analyst gains deeper knowledge of the patient (see Chapter
Four for more details). Jacobs wonders if work with physically traumatised patients is more often associated with somatic resonances in
the analyst. He also allows for individual variations within analysts
themselves.

> While it seems self-evident that an analyst, while listening, uti-
> lizes his entire self in the process and that bodily movements are
> an integral and essential part of the "analyzing instrument", the
> degree to which bodily reactions are both available and useful to
> the analyst unquestionably differs from individual to individual.
> In some analysts who have had significant experiences of bodily
> illness or trauma, or who perhaps for other reasons of an innate or
> experiential kind have a highly cathected body ego, there may be
> an increased capacity to utilize bodily responses in their analytic
> work. In others, whose development along different lines may have
> led to an increased investment in the visual or auditory spheres or
> in fantasy formation, or in individuals in whom defensive opera-
> tions may be directed against awareness of bodily sensations, such
> experiences may play a lesser role in the analyst's use of himself.
> (Ibid., p. 116)

Lest this gives the impression that in "listening subjectively", Jacobs
relies solely upon his bodily experiences, I hasten to add that he cites
numerous clinical vignettes where a passing thought, a childhood memory, the discovery of his wearing mismatched clothes, and a strong but
unexplained surge of emotion within himself became a clue to the deeper
messages emanating from the patient. He asserts that contact with such
elements of one's subjectivity "helps illuminate preconscious material
in the patient that is rising towards consciousness" (2007, p. 104). Jacobs

(1992, 2007) credits the origins of his thinking to Otto Isakower's (1963a, 1963b) concept of "analytic instrument". This refers to

> a joint creation of patient and analyst. Assembled in, and existing only, during the analytic hour, it might concretely be imagined as a brain containing two halves. One half belongs to the patient, the other half to the analyst. In the analytic session as both analyst and patient loosen their ties to the external world and enter into a slightly altered state of consciousness—essentially a condition of daydreaming—these two halves come together in a temporary union, a bridge is built, and unconscious messages can flow between them. In this state of mind, which the analyst must consciously employ—and, arguably due in large measure to this state of mind—it is highly likely that the analyst's subjective experiences will be meaningfully and importantly related to communications from the patient. (2007, p. 100)

One issue that also needs inclusion in this section on listening subjectively pertains to the concept of "projective identification" (Klein, 1946). This is a process that begins in early infancy and consists of parts of the rudimentary self being split off and projected into an external object. The latter then becomes identified with the repudiated part as well as internally controlled by it. While starting out as a developmental process parallel to introjection, projective identification can come to serve many defensive purposes. These include attempted fusion with external objects to avoid the existential burden of separateness, extrusion of bad internal objects that cause persecutory anxieties, and preservation of endangered good aspects of the self by depositing them into others. Bion (1967) extended the notion of projective identification to include the depositing of unthinkable thoughts ("beta elements", in his terminology) into a receptive other who can metabolise them and return them to the subject in a piecemeal manner.

Within the clinical situation, the use of "projective identification" on the patient's part leads the analyst to experience what the patient cannot bear to feel or think. The frequent development of violently negative countertransference while working with borderline patients has been elucidated by Kernberg (1975, 1984, 1992) in great detail; he has also described the technical strategies consequent upon such feelings. However, the deployment of projective identification is not limited to borderline patients. Individuals with other severe personality disorders also tend to use this defence mechanism. And its impact shows up in the turbulent subjectivity of the treating clinician. The analyst working with a narcissistic patient, for instance, experiences feelings of inferiority and even shame (about his clothes, office, language skills, knowledge of world affairs, etc.); such feelings constitute not only the "natural" responses to someone's grandiosity but, on a deeper level, reflect an identification with the projected shame-laden parts of the patient. Similarly, schizoid patients who have been coldly hated and wished "gone" by the parents often deposit their "alive" aspects into the analyst who begins to feel an increase in his vitality and goodness (Kramer & Akhtar, 1988). The analyst who "listens" to himself and pays close attention to his subjective goings-on can learn a lot about his patients.

Empathic listening

The exact opposite of "projective identification" is empathy. The former involves the patient's actively putting something into the analyst's mind. The latter involves the analyst's actively seeking to resonate with the patient's experience. To understand this well, we need to return to Fliess's (1942) remarkable paper, "The Metapsychology of the Analyst". Introducing the term "trial identification", Fliess explains the process by which one comes to understand what someone else is actually saying. In order to empathise with someone, one *"introjects this object transiently, and projects the introject again on to the object*. This alone enables him in the end to square a perception from without and one from within" (p. 212, italics in the original). Applying this scheme to the patient's transference-based strivings in the clinical situation, Fliess describes:

> the following four phases in this "metabolic process": (1) the analyst is the object of the striving; (2) he identifies with the subject, the patient; (3) he becomes this subject himself; (4) he projects the striving, after he has "tasted" it himself, back on the patient and so finds himself in the possession of the inside knowledge of its nature, having thereby acquired the emotional basis for his interpretation. (Ibid, p. 215)

Fliess allows the space for the analyst's own reverie but declares that it should not extend beyond "conditioned daydreaming", that is, the analyst's daydreaming should be triggered only by the patient's material, not by his own personal preoccupations. Resolute in his attention to the patient's spoken words (and their associated affects), he states that the analyst "restricts his vigilance almost exclusively to one sphere, that of hearing. The eye serves as but an accessory to the ear; smell is almost, the sense of touch completely, excluded, for he reciprocates his patient's motor restrictions" (ibid., p. 216).

Greenson (1960), another major contributor to the empathic perspective on analytic listening, added further nuances to the topic. Listening alone is not enough, he says. The analyst must possess the ability for controlled and reversible regressions in his ego functions (see also Nichols, 2009). A temporary decathexis of one's own self-image is also necessary. Only then is it possible to shift "from listening and observing from the outside to listening and feeling from the inside" (p. 420). Greenson traces the origins of empathy in the early mother-child relationship and holds that male analysts must come to terms with their "motherly component" (p. 422) in order to be truly empathic.

Whether empathic listening—as opposed to, say, objective listening—can more rapidly yield meaningful information about the patient is also addressed by Greenson.

> Empathy and intuition are related. Both are special methods of gaining quick and deep understanding. One empathizes to reach feelings; one uses intuition to get ideas. Empathy is to affects and impulses what intuition is to thinking. Empathy often leads to intuition. The "Aha" reaction in intuited. You arrive at the feelings and pictures via empathy, but intuition sets off the signal in the analytic ego that you have hit it. Intuition picks up the clues that empathy gathers. Empathy is essentially a function of the experiencing ego, whereas intuition comes from the analyzing ego. (p. 422)

While showing great interest in the empathic perspective, Greenson largely maintained an eclectic approach towards analytic listening, moving deftly between various forms of listening though without explicitly registering such latitude. In contrast, Heinz Kohut and Evelyne Schwaber made the empathic form of listening the centrepiece of their approach. This reflects what Strenger (1989) has termed the "romantic vision" of psychoanalysis. Founded largely on Goethe's and Rousseau's humanistic thoughts, such a perspective sees man as striving towards becoming a cohesive self. Development aims at a self which consists of a continuous flow from ambitions to ideas, from a sense of vitality towards goals which are experienced as intrinsically valuable. Mental suffering is the result of the failure of the environment to fulfill the self-object function and the patient's symptoms are the desperate attempt to fill the vacuum in his depleted self. The analyst's attitude towards the patient is one of trust in his humanity and the analyst takes the side of joy and vitality. The ethic is romantic: maturity and mental health consist in the ability to sustain enthusiasm and a sense of meaning. (p. 601)

That noted, let us return now to Kohut's and Schwaber's contributions. Kohut, a classical Freudian and most likely an "objective listener" for most of his early analytic career, took a dramatic turn in the late 1970s. In his *The Restoration of the Self* (1977), he placed the self as a superordinate constellation and downgraded drives and defences from being the self's originators to its constituents. His language also changed. The grandiose self, idealised parent imago, narcissistic transferences, and transmuting internalisation (Kohut, 1971) gave way to nuclear goals, nuclear ambitions, selective inclusion, and self-object phenomena (Kohut, 1977). To put a final stamp on this radical shift, Kohut (1982) declared that his "self-psychology has freed itself from the distorted view of psychological man espoused by traditional analysis" (p. 402).

All this had a clear impact on the listening perspective he came to embrace. The analyst's empathic immersion in his patient's subjective experience now became the cornerstone of his technique. In a series of papers and a posthumously published monograph, Kohut (1979, 1980, 1982, 1984) elaborated upon the reparative function of the analyst's empathy and the need to listen—solely—from the patient's point of view. His widely read (and gossiped about)[5] paper "Two Analyses of Mr Z" (Kohut, 1979) laid these ideas out in eloquent details.

The proposal of listening from the patient's perspective then found a fervent advocate in Schwaber. In contributions spanning three decades (Schwaber, 1981, 1983, 1995, 1998, 2005, 2007), she has championed the cause of empathic listening. Taking the monumental shift, in early psychoanalysis from seduction theory to fantasy-based neurosogenesis as her starting point, Schwaber laments that the listening perspective of many analysts has not undergone a corresponding change. They do not seem to heed Freud's (1917) declaration that *"in the world of neuroses, it is psychical reality which is the decisive kind"* (p. 368, italics in the original) and continue to talk the patient's "misperceptions" and "distortions"—which they, presumably, as superior arbiters of reality, seek to correct. In contrast, Schwaber proposes a:

> mode of attunement which attempts to maximize a singular focus on the patient's subjective reality, seeking all possible cues to ascertain it. Vigilantly guarding against the imposition of the analyst's point of view, the role of the analyst and of the surround, as perceived and experienced by the patient, is recognized as intrinsic to that reality; the observer is a part of the field observed. As a scientific modality, empathy employs our cognitive, perceptual, as well as affective capacities ... The analyst's empathy draws upon modalities which are significant components of the essentials of parental empathy—attunement to and recognition of the perceptive and experiential states of another. (1981, p. 378)

The shift in perspective from listening from the outside to listening from the patient's perspective has profound implications for the analyst's view of the patient and of the clinical process itself.

> Transference, the inner representation of the past amalgamated to the present, is then not viewed as a distortion, for this would imply that there is a reality more "correct" than the patient's psychic view of us, which we as "outside" observers could ascertain. Understood as the property of the system, psychic experience is not separate from its context; the "transference" is inseparable from the "real" .... Thus the reality, for each of us, represents only our psychic view—even of ourselves—the notion of an attainable certainty of an ultimate knowable reality must be regarded as illusory, a perspective often most difficult to sustain, perhaps because it is disquieting. (Schwaber, 1983, p. 522)

Schwaber emphasises that the analyst's task is to seek the inner world of the patient and there is no better way to do so than to listen from the patient's perspective. The analyst must avoid foreclosure, the temptation to guide, and to help the patient see "hidden meanings". His recognising the inner state of the patient—his "getting it"—is in itself good enough. Feeling understood renders the patient capable of increasing the exposure of his inner world and this, in turn, enhances psychic coherence and self-regulating organisation. "The search to 'get it' is the route, and the goal, enabling the therapeutic action" (Schwaber, 2007, p. 38).

Nosek (2009) advances this discourse to a higher level. In his remarkable plenary address to the 45th IPA Congress held in Chicago, IL, he proposed that interpretation is, in the end, a form of psychic violence and psychoanalysis is essentially about helping the patient reveal himself to himself and to the analyst. Nosek details such radical reformulation of the fundamentals of our technique in the following passage.

> If we are prepared to forego the violence of knowledge, if we are not incited by the urgency of ontology and the power of positivism, we encounter the territory of hospitality: this means receiving the foreigner as such, allowing him his own existence. This gesture, configured as goodness, does not ennoble or exalt me; its character comes from the infinite to be received, unraveling my possibilities … For us psychoanalysts, this is a radical hierarchical reflection: psychoanalysis is no longer a talking cure but a listening cure. (p. 145)[6]

Intersubjective listening

This perspective is derived from Harry Stack Sullivan's (1947, 1953) interpersonal view of psychoanalysis which declares that self is nothing but a collection of reflective appraisals and anxiety can only occur in an interpersonal context. As a result, the intersubjective listening has a threefold theoretical foundation: (i) clinical work as embedded in the dynamic interplay between two selves, (ii) all the analytic material (including transference and countertransference) is co-constructed, and (iii) analytic listening is a shared process. A challenge to the positivist scientific orientation of "classical" analysis, the intersubjective paradigm proposes that no mental phenomena can be properly understood if approached as entities existing solipsistically within the patient's mind. The analyst's perception of the patient's thoughts, feelings, and fantasies, etc., is always shaped by the analyst's subjectivity. Therefore, the patient's psychology—the "material" for analysis—is itself co-constructed.

Intersubjective clinicians (Benjamin, 1995, 2004, 2007; Hoffman, 1991; Ogden, 1992, 1994; Spezzano, 1993; Stolorow, Brandchaft & Atwood, 1987, 1992) regard their method to more truly reflect the nature of human psychology; it is less mechanistic and less likely to reify mental life. They view the clinical process as a dialectical interplay between the patient's subjective reality and the analyst's subjective reality as well as the interaction of these two psychic realities with the intersubjective reality they create together. These analysts put emphasis upon reciprocal listening, that is, how the analyst is listening to the patient *and* how the patient is registering (and interpreting) what the analyst is saying *and* how that alters what the analyst would say next, and so on. This is where Ogden's (1994) concept of the "analytic third" comes in. This term refers to the intersubjective experience which is a product of a unique dialectic generated between the individual subjectivities of the analyst and the analysand within the analytic setting. The "analytic third" is not a "structure" insofar as it is forever fresh, being created, destroyed, and re-created in every passing moment of the clinical hour. There is more here to consider. "The analytic third is a creation of the analyst and the analysand, and at the same time, the analyst and the analysand (qua analyst and analysand) are created by the analytic third" (ibid., p. 93). This affects how one views the analytic process itself. According to Ogden:

> Analysis is not simply a method of uncovering the hidden; it is more importantly a process of creating the analytic subject who had not previously existed. For example, the analysand's history is not uncovered, it is created in the transference-countertransference and is perpetually in a state of flux as the intersubjectivity of the analytic process evolves and is interpreted by analyst and analysand (see Schafer, 1976, 1978). In this way the analytic subject is created by, and exists in an ever-evolving state in the dynamic intersubjectivity of the analytic process: the subject of psychoanalysis takes shape in the interpretive space *between* analyst and analysand. (ibid., p. 47, italics in the original)

The intersubjective perspective regards the analyst's affective state as an active constructing force of the transference and countertransference. It is not merely a response to the patient's material but a co-creation of the two members of the clinical dyad. Viewing all communications of each partner as designed to elicit responses from the other, the intersubjective approach harks back to the child's early curiosity about (and the desire to connect with) the mother's feelings; this is seen to repeat in the form of the analysand's curiosity about the analyst. Aron (1991) and Mitchell (1991) argue against considering such curiosities drive-based. Such interpretations, according to them, thwart the developmental strivings of the patient.

Benjamin (2004, 2007) takes the notion of the "analytic third" further, delineating three subcategories of it: (i) "primordial third", emanating from the musical or rhythmic exchange of sounds and gestures in the mother-child relationship and showing up in the analytic situation as accommodation, attunement, and regularity of the dyad's relatedness, (ii) "symbolic third", which involves more nuanced procedures and expectations of narrative recognition of separateness, and negotiation, and (iii) "moral third", the agreed-upon principles of "the valuing of truth, striving for accommodation, responsibility and respect for the other, and faith in the process of rupture and repair" (2007, p. 99). This last-mentioned principle demands that the analyst listen most carefully to himself and try to ascertain how he might be contributing to the disruption of the clinical dialogue at any given moment. Analytic listening is ideally directed equally to the patient's subjectivity, the analyst's subjectivity, and the intersubjectivity they create together. In fact, the first two designations are inherently suspect, since the "third" creates them while being created by them as well. In essence, nothing can be listened to without taking the impact of the relationship between the analyst and the patient into account.

Putting the four models together

It seems desirable—indeed, tempting—to seamlessly blend the four models of analytic listening described here. Synthesis of such elegance would reduce theoretical ambiguity and diminish the technical necessity of making choices and exercising judgment. However, this conceptual pastiche—assuming that it can be assembled—carries the risk of oversimplification on both theoretical and clinical planes. It is therefore best to not force a union and instead let the models stand as they are without overlooking their potential harmony and confluence. In starting this way, one might even end up with the discovery of some deeper unifying pattern after all. First, though, let us take the following points about these models into account.

- The four models need not only a proper space in the external sense of the word but also "the internal analytic setting" (Parsons, 2007) for their optimal unfolding. The latter concept refers to "a psychic arena in which reality is defined by such concepts as symbolism, fantasy, transference, and unconscious meaning …. The internal setting defines and protects an area of the analyst's mind where whatever happens, including whatever happens to the external setting, can be considered by a psychoanalytic viewpoint" (p. 1443).
- The four models have areas of overlap. "Objective listening", for instance, might lead to a great sense of empathy with the patient and, conversely, "empathic listening" might benefit by objectively registering each and every facet of the patient's narrative. "Subjective listening" seems an essential component of "intersubjective listening". Moreover, the latter might actually require a certain objectivity in order to be truly comprehensive. Smith (1999) notes that "Subjectivity and objectivity are both necessary pathways to knowledge and are dependent upon each other. Any form of looking or listening does to some extent preclude another, but to speak solely from a subjective or an objective perspective represents a regression in thinking to a form of naïve objectivism or naïve subjectivism" (p. 465).
- The four models described here might not be exhaustive of the ways of listening employed by analysts. There might be hybrid forms that use an admixture of these approaches. The manner of listening recommended by Arlow (1995) is a prime example of this. On the one hand, its governing principle is that the analyst must demonstrate to the patient "how present-day experience may be misinterpreted in terms of derivatives of persistent unconscious fantasies from the past" (p. 221). This is reflective of "objective listening". On the other hand, Arlow recommends that the analyst must "try to understand the message behind the manifest productions … [and] be alert to the connecting thread that runs through the patient's productions" (p. 222). This is closer to "empathic listening". Going one step further, Arlow notes that the analyst must observe the impact of his statements upon the patient and "the interchange itself is subject to examination and interpretation" (p. 229), thus coming closer to the intersubjective perspective described above. Arlow is not alone in employing such

hybrid forms of listening. Gill (1979, 1994), with his dual emphasis upon transference interpretation and the need to acknowledge the plausibility of patients' perceptions, also seems to blend the "objective" and the "intersubjective" approaches to listening. In his technical recommendations regarding enactments, Boesky (1990), too, straddles the "objective" and "intersubjective" approaches.

- The four models of listening give rise to different questions in the analyst's mind.[7] "Objective listening" directs one's attention towards syntax, shifts in the direction of association, parapraxes, and so on. "Subjective listening" intensifies vigilance towards the countertransference experience. "Empathic listening" facilitates a deeper grasp of the patient's narrative, especially in its conscious and preconscious aspects. "Intersubjective listening" spurs curiosity about the two partners' influence upon each other and upon their mutuality itself.
- The four models of listening are implicit in Schlesinger's (2003) wise recommendation that the analyst must learn to listen from several modes at once. These include: (i) listening contextually, or taking into account the patient's history, the course of treatment so far, and the realities of the patient's current life, (ii) listening naïvely and without preconception, (iii) listening to intent rather than to content alone, (iv) listening empathically, and (v) listening in the light of transference and countertransference.
- The four models of listening yield different sorts of data which, working in unison, can enhance the understanding of the patient. In the same vein, Spencer and Balter (1990) underscore the complementarity of the "introspective" and the "behavioural" modes of observation in psychoanalysis. In the former, the analyst puts himself in the position of the analysand and derives clinical understanding from the latter's perspective. In the latter, the analyst adopts the "view of a spectator, without regard to the subject's own thoughts or feelings" (p. 402). The two methods, often yielding different sets of information, modify each other in the service of deepening the grasp of the analysand's mental functioning.

This last-mentioned point can become the springboard for a synthesis, after all. Perhaps the "objective" (more so) and "intersubjective" (less so) models of listening constitute what Killingmo (1989) has called "sceptical listening" and the "empathic" and "subjective" forms of listening might constitute what he has termed "credulous" listening. "Credulous listening" focuses upon *what* the patient is saying, "sceptical listening" on *how* the patient is saying what he is saying. The analyst who is listening credulously pays great attention to the patient's preoccupation and complaints; he finds them meaningful in their own right and is not in a rush to unmask their meanings. The analyst who is listening sceptically is attuned to what is hidden behind the patient's manifest content; he eschews what is on the surface and wishes both the parties in the clinical situation to delve deeper. Klauber has captured the implications of this difference in the following succinct passage.

> The degree to which analysis of conscious and preconscious attitudes should be allowed to shade off into discussion of the patient's problems depends upon the theoretical orientation of the psychoanalyst. For those analysts for whom interpretation is oriented to the ego, it seems inevitable for the accurate clarification of the unconscious conflict that the conscious and preconscious derivatives of the unconscious should be fully explored. Other psychoanalysts might dispute the appropriateness of the discussion of the patient's problems—of which some analysts approve—and consider it a degradation of psychoanalytic technique. (1968, p. 137)

Contrast this last statement with what Schlesinger says regarding the tension between listening to the surface and depth of the patient's material.

> What is importantly unconscious and determinative at the moment, though it may derive ultimately from sources far from consciousness, will generally be represented in more superficial manifestations that are accessible to the knowledgeable observer. (2003, p. 118)

This underscores the importance of listening credulously. The fact is that such listening helps establish a sense of mutuality and of being "on the same page". It provides a glimpse of the patient's ego functioning in the external world and of the issues that preoccupy him, even though they might be chosen because of their significance in terms of unconscious conflict. Such attention to "surface material" also gives a hint of transferences that are about to unfold or are already going on. Sceptical listening, in contrast, is essentially deconstructive in nature. It consists of the following aspects.

- Listening to the *omissions* in the narrative (e.g., an individual talking in detail about a house he is purchasing but never mentioning its price, a woman talking about her boyfriend but omitting his name) helps discern pockets of anxiety and transference-based resistances.
- Listening to *slips of the tongue*, and *mispronunciations* that are not based on unfamiliarity with the language being spoken, and *other verbal gaffes* of the patient also provides access to his unconscious functioning at that moment.
- Listening to the *intonations and points of emphasis* (e.g., "*All* I want from my husband is a little attention", "I *really* do love my mother") yields useful information regarding characterological styles and self-deceptions that individuals are often compelled to deploy.
- Listening to *pauses* can also be informative (see Chapter Two for more details). Often the clause of the sentence added after a pause turns out to be defensive against the anxiety the first part of the sentence has stirred up (e.g., "Sometimes I think of committing suicide" followed by a pause, and then the phrase, "Well, not really").
- Listening to *negations and unsolicited disavowals* reveals the distressing deeper content (e.g., "The last person who comes to my mind in this connection is my father", "Look, I'm not competing with you").
- Listening to the patient's *sighs and grunts* permits access to areas of pain, anxiety, and resistance. Attention to such sonic cues yields even richer data when an eye is also kept on the patient's bodily movements during the session (McLaughlin, 1992).

The developmentally derived prototypes of the "credulous" and "sceptical" listening styles are divergent (see below). And the same might apply to the four models outlined here. "Objective listening" seems more paternal and "empathic listening" more maternal in nature. "Subjective listening" and "intersubjective listening" fall somewhere between these two poles, with the former being closer to the paternal and the latter to the maternal end of the relational spectrum. Indeed, the proponents of "empathic", "subjective", and "intersubjective" models link the style of their attunement to the mother's early attention to her child. Schwaber (1981, 1983), Jacobs (1991), and Ogden (1994) invoke the observations of Sander (1975), Burlingham (1967), and Winnicott

(1953), respectively, for this purpose. Interestingly, no one mentions the father-child dialogue as a prototype for listening in psychoanalysis, even though the echoes of this relationship are discernable in the "objective listening" model. This lopsided approach is rectified in the developmental model described below.

A developmental postscript

The technical polarities of listening with credulousness versus listening with scepticism seem to have their respective developmental prototypes in the maternal and paternal styles of relating to young children. Herzog's (1984) elucidation of the "homeostatic" and "disruptive" attunements of parents to their growing child is especially illuminating in this context. Through video-monitored child-observational studies, Herzog has demonstrated that mothers usually join in with a toddler in his or her ongoing play, thus giving the child a "continuity of being" (Winnicott, 1965, p. 54), validity, and harmony with the environment ("homeostatic attunement"). Fathers, on the contrary, characteristically disrupt the playing toddler's equilibrium by cajoling him or her into *joining them* in a new activity ("disruptive attunement"). Homeostatic attunement has affirming qualities necessary for the sustenance and consolidation of self-experience. Disruptive attunement has enhancing qualities necessary for broadening and deepening of self-experience. The influence of the two types of attunements is additive and contributes to the fluid solidity of a healthy self-experience. Herzog further observed that fathers distract the child from the game he is playing only when the mother is with the child. In her absence, and especially with younger children, fathers, too, start playing the child's own game (i.e., resort to homeostatic attunement). This suggests that homeostatic attunement is an experiential prerequisite for disruptive attunement.

Extrapolating these developmental observations to the clinical situation suggests the following. The analyst's credulous listening and his "holding" (Winnicott, 1960a) and "affirmative" (Killingmo, 1989) interventions are akin to the maternal "homeostatic attunement" insofar as they, too, aim to validate, strengthen, and stabilise the self-experience. The analyst's scepticism regarding the patient's conscious material and his unmasking interpretive interventions seem akin to the paternal "disruptive attunement" insofar as these cause cognitive expansion by introducing new material into the patient's awareness.

Herzog's conclusion that homeostatic attunement is a prerequisite for disruptive attunement also finds a parallel in the clinical situation wherein the analyst's holding and affirmative (i.e., homeostatic) functions must be securely in place in order for his interpretive (i.e., disruptive) efforts to be fruitful. The patient's inner sense of the analytic relationship must be stable (or should be stabilised) for him or her to utilise the destabilising impact of interpretation which, by definition, brings something new to the patient's attention. The patient must possess or be helped to possess a "safety feeling" (Sandler, 1960, p. 4) before the risk of encountering the repudiated aspects of his self-experience. Couched in the developmental metaphor, the analyst's exercise of maternal functions seems to be a prerequisite for his or her exercise of paternal functions. Restated in clinical terms, credulous listening must prepare the ground for listening with scepticism.

Designating such maternal and paternal interventions as "two poles of therapeutic technique", Wright traces their respective origins to Freud and Winnicott.

> Freud, it seems to me, stands for the father with his forbidding and prohibitions. Winnicott stands for the mother and her caring, nurturing, and loving. Freud is the mediator of the reality principle to which the child must adapt; Winnicott is the protector of a kinder, more lenient space, which keeps reality, to some extent, at bay. (1991, p. 280)

In Wright's view, analysis involves a renewal of the process of psychic formation. It provides the space within which new forms or symbols of the self may be created. However, for fully separated and representative symbols, as well as less separated and iconic symbols in the human discourse to emerge, be understood, and coalesce, the analytic technique requires both maternal and internal elements. The maternal element (holding, facilitating, enabling, and surviving) "posits faith in the background process. Things will happen if you wait" (p. 283). The paternal element (searching, confronting, deciphering, and interpreting) underlies the analyst's scepticism, his struggles with the patient's resistances, his confrontations with the turbulent world of intrapsychic conflict. Wright goes on to suggest that the two modes of intervention might be appropriate at different times and foster different modes of symbolising. Analytic listening is not static and shifts according to the patient's structural level at a given moment (Killingmo, 1989), degree of psychic organisation in general (Wright, 1991), and the ever-changing tone and direction of the patient's free association (Miller & Aisentein, 2004).

In general, maternal holding of the physically banished elements has to precede a meaningful looking at them with the aim of further self-understanding. "Containing holding" is a prior condition for "trans-formative looking" (Wright, 1991, p. 300). Moreover, the maternal and paternal elements of technique "provide a point and counterpoint in analysis between two styles and two visions and neither wins the day completely" (ibid., p. 280). It should also be remembered that such maternal and paternal attributes are not gender-based in a literal sense. There are male analysts who seem more maternal and female analysts who seem more paternal in technique. At the same time, it is true that most analysts, regardless of their actual gender, possess both these attributes and strive to incorporate them in their technical approaches.

Wright's bringing together of the Freud-Winnicott technical schism seems to have seamless underpinnings in Herzog's (1984) develop-mental observations. In the end, it all boils down to placing agreement before disagreement, consolidation before deconstruction, empathy before insight, affirmation before interpretation, and "mother" before "father", while recognising that *both* experiences are as necessary in psychoanalytic treatment as they are in the course of development.

Concluding remarks

After Freud's (1912e) seminal recommendations on analytic listening, there developed a protracted silence on the matter. The textbooks of psychoanalysis (Moore & Fine, 1995; Nersessian & Kopf, 1996; Person, Cooper, & Gabbard, 2005) and monographs devoted to psychoanalytic technique (Etchegoyen, 2005; Fenichel, 1941; Greenson, 1967; Volkan, 2010) published over subsequent years said little about the nature of analytic listening. The PEP (Psychoanalytic Electronic Publishing) web[8] reveals that all twenty-eight papers with the words "analytic listening" in their title were published after 1980, or nearly seven decades after Freud enunciated his views. The reasons for both the long silence and the sudden spurt of interest are unclear. The difficulty in coming out of the master's shadow and the increasing theoretical pluralism in psy-choanalysis might account for these, respectively.

By bringing together the pertinent literature that has emerged, I have delineated four models of analytic listening, namely, (i) objective listening, (ii) subjective listening, (iii) empathic listening, and (iv) intersubjective listening. Each has its theoretical anchors and its technical yields. After elucidating these, I have attempted to discern the areas of overlap in these models and also noted some hybrid forms that can easily fall between partisan cracks. I have also traced the developmental prototypes of various forms of listening and linked the "credulous listening/affirmative intervention" and "sceptical listening/interpretive intervention" dichotomy of analytic technique with the maternal and paternal forms of relating to children, respectively. Putting extra premium on neither of these and underscoring the utility of both, I have opted for a technique that oscillates, in an informed manner, between the two ends of this developmental-clinical spectrum (for further details, see Akhtar, 2000). An optimal blend of the two is what makes analytic listening properly attuned and ultimately useful to the patient. Such listening is directed to the patient's words as well as to his non-verbal communications and silences.

Notes

1. Greater effort to listen deeply is, at times, necessitated by the nature of the patient's psychopathology. Ferenczi's (1929) recommendations for dealing with people who, as children, have been unwelcomed and hated, are pertinent in this context. Gammill (1980) also notes that in dealing with schizoid patients, "very considerable attentiveness was necessary to pick up even the faintest indications of affect and of material linked with the remains of [an] authentic and personal self" (p. 376).

2. Analysts also vary in their choice of "listening aids", the things or activities that anchor their mind in one place and thus permit free-floating attention to the patient's material. Some analysts take notes. Others doodle or draw. Some (mostly outside the United States) smoke cigarettes or cigars. Others knit or crochet. Some place their chairs in a way that permits them to see the patient's face. Others close their eyes. A few have their dogs and cats present during the clinical hour. And so on.

3. Meissner (2000) also notes that analytic listening is not naïve, but rather prepared and focused. He says that "Listening to theoretical models rather than to the patient is obvious mishearing … or better, 'mis-listening'; but at the same time, listening takes place partly by means

of such models, and cannot occur without them. If theoretical models have their limits, so does naïve or mindless acceptance of the patient's viewpoint" (p. 325).

4. The fact that Klein (1926) regarded child's play as the equivalent to an adult's free association is better known than that she held the opposite to be true as well.

5. There are many (e.g., Cocks, 1994; Giovacchini, 2000) who believe that Mr Z was actually Kohut himself and what he reported as two analyses were actually reflections upon his analysis and his self-generated understanding.

6. I had earlier (Akhtar, 2007) used the term "listening cure" but, in a more modest way, suggested that psychoanalysis is both a listening and a talking cure.

7. This is akin to Pine's (1988) "four psychologies of psychoanalysis". These conceptually separable perspectives include those of drives, ego, object relations, and self. They overlap but each adds something different to the understanding of development, psychopathology, and technique.

8. The PEP Archive (1871-2008) contains the complete text of forty-six premier journals in psychoanalysis, seventy classic psychoanalytic books, and the full text and editorial notes of the twenty-four volumes of the *Standard Edition* as well as the eighteen volume German *Gesammelte Werke*. The PEP Archive spans 137 publication years and contains the full text of articles whose source ranges from 1871 through 2008. There are approximately 75,000 articles and 8,728 figures that originally resided on 1,449 volumes with a total of over *650,000 printed pages*.

CHAPTER TWO

Listening to silence

Silence is ubiquitous in human dialogue and is therefore bound to make its appearance in the analytic exchange as well.[1] Having consistently attracted the attention of poets and philosophers (both Western and Eastern), silence has proven itself to be a topic of intrigue and a potential key to knowledge. And both intrigue and knowledge matter deeply to psychoanalysis. The relevance of silence to psychoanalysis becomes unmistakably clear when one takes into account that silence between two (or more) human beings can signify a vast range of feelings and psychic configurations. Zeligs notes that silence can convey:

> agreement, disagreement, pleasure, displeasure, fear, anger, or tranquility. The silence could be a sign of contentment, mutual understanding, and compassion. Or, it might indicate emptiness and complete lack of affect. Human silence can radiate warmth or

cast a chill. At one moment, it may be laudatory and accepting; in the next, it can be cutting and contemptuous. Silence may express poise, smugness, snobbishness, taciturnity, or humility. Silence may mean yes or no. It may be giving or receiving, object-directed or narcissistic. Silence may be the sign of defeat or the mask of mastery. When life-and-death situations are being sweated through, there is little occasion for words. Silence may be discreet or indiscreet. A tactful silence serves to prevent the expression of inappropriate thoughts and feelings. (1961, pp. 8–9)

Humbled by such eloquence, I nonetheless wish to move along and offer some further insights regarding silence, especially as it appears in the clinical situation. I would begin by delineating eight types of silences along with a "translation" of the drive-based and object-related scenarios associated with each of them. Following this, I will make a brief foray into the sociocultural realm and elucidate a variety of silences encountered in that context. Then I will return to the clinical arena and highlight the various functions of the patient's silence and the technical strategies helpful to deal with them. I will also comment on the positive and negative impact of the analyst's silence upon the clinical process. Following this, I will discuss the concept of "mutual silence" during clinical work. I will conclude by summarising this material and by raising questions about aspects of silence that might still lie beyond our grasp and remain untouched by our verbal fumblings.

Varieties of silence

While cognizant of the fact that the categories of silence I am about to propose might neither be completely exclusive of each other nor exhaustive of the phenomena under investigation, I nonetheless find it heuristically as well as technically useful to view silence along the following typology.

Structural silence

Since "structure" merely implies a relatively predictable and recurring set of processes, it is both quizzical and understandable to speak of "structural silence". It is quizzical because how can something become organised if it is quiet and not adequately mentalised. It is understandable because aspects of mind do exist that are entirely process-oriented and not content-based. An illustration of this is Winnicott's (1960a) concept of "true self". Denoting the "going-on-being" (Winnicott, 1956) and un-thought psychosomatic continuity of existence, the "true self" is indescribable. It reflects living authentically with a lambent corporeality and unimpeded psychic life (both operating in peaceful unison); indeed the essence of true self is "*incommunicado*" (Winnicott, 1963, p. 187).

Another illustration of "structural silence" or silent structures is constituted by the "area of creation" (Balint, 1968). In this realm of psychic experience, there is no external or internal object present. "The subject is on his own and his main concern is to produce something out of himself; this something to be produced may be an object but not necessarily so" (p. 24). Besides artistic creation, mathematics, and philosophy, this mental sphere includes "understanding something or somebody, and last but not least, two highly important phenomena: the early phases of becoming—bodily or mentally—'ill', and spontaneous recovery from that 'illness'" (p. 24). Even when the subject is without an object, he is not entirely alone. He is most probably with "pre-objects", dim fragments of non-self representation that congeal into treated objects only after much preconscious work. The "area of creation" appears in the clinical situation, at times, when the patient is silent and pensive. Such a patient might not be running "away" from disturbing mental contents but might be running "towards" the state of having tangible mental content. This type of silence need not be ruptured by an "intervention"; the analyst must wait patiently till the patient "returns" from his reverie with a "solution" to his malady of the moment.

A third example of "structured silence" is constituted by the psychic material under the domain of "primal repression" (Breuer & Freud, 1895d). There is little preconscious representation of the material under "primal repression" and the prefix "primal" (as opposed to "primary") underscores not only the early but the ubiquitous nature of the phenomenon in human experience. "Primal repression" is associated with the non-verbal period of infancy; the elements under it can not be verbally recalled but only be relived. In Frank's (1969) terminology, this is "the unrememberable and the unforgettable" (p. 48) substrate of the human psyche.

Unmentalised silence

We know from Bion (1962a, 1962b) and, more recently, from Fonagy and Target (1997) that it takes the maternal processing of a child's spontaneous, even though incoherent and "un-thinkable" psychic material to cohere in sustainable and intelligible thoughts. In Bion's terms, this is turning beta elements into alpha elements or incomprehensible and vague affect-sensations into formed narratives that can be reflected upon. It is this maternal attitude that ultimately bestows the gift of ability to think about one's mental goings-on. In its absence or pronounced limitation—such as in the case of a "dead mother" (Green, 1983)—the child grows up to be an individual who has little to say in response to others' thoughts and even as a follow-up of his own inescapable spontaneity. In clinical situations, we see such individuals interrupt their half-hearted forays into free association with an exasperated "anyway", "so that's it", "I have nothing more to say about this", followed by a sigh. It is as if they have run out of ideas and are staring—puzzled and clueless—at the abyss of wordlessness. Interventional strategies with such patients falter if their "silence" is regarded as a resistance. It is more productive to gently encourage them to "think" more. The analyst, for instance, might say to such a patient "Next time, instead of saying that 'I have nothing more to say about it', try saying 'I have nothing more that *I know* to say about it'," or "The next time you are about to end what you are saying by sighing and saying 'anyway', and then changing the topic, try saying 'I was about to say anyway but will try to go on and see what more—even it seemingly unrelated to the topic—can come to mind'." Such "educative" measures convey to the patient that the analyst is not only interested in the un-mined (pun unintended) areas of his mental field but genuinely believes that the patient can develop the ability to look at this realm himself.[2]

Defensive silence

This is the most recognised type of silence in terms of clinical psychoanalysis. Such silence might appear spontaneously and is then a response to the emergent unacceptable wishes and fantasies in the patient. It serves to keep in abeyance those drives, drive-directives, and the transference wishes consequent upon them that are felt morally repugnant or shameful by the patient. For instance, a patient talking about his drive to succeed and be famous might suddenly stop talking. Anxiety takes over and his ability to free-associate is transiently compromised. He seems to have lost his train of thought. Gentle encouragement, along with some "defense analysis" (A. Freud, 1936) might result in the patient's revealing that he wishes to win a Nobel Prize. In turn, such revelation makes it possible to analyse the patient's motives in this regard but also, and perhaps more important, his transference-based fears of rejection and criticism for his ambition. Seeming to hinder the progress of analysis, the silence of resistance affords the analyst a wonderful opportunity to bring deep and conflicted material to the surface.

Guilt, shame, and fear of retaliation are, however, not the only motivators of silence in the service of resistance. Loving and feeling loved can also appear threatening, especially to schizoid and masochistic patients, and become the subject of mental erasure. Just as the patient begins to feel loved, anxiety rises and drowns the capacity for verbalisation.

Finally, there is the phenomenon of deliberate withholding. Here the patient refuses to share with the analyst something that he knows (e.g., an extramarital affair, cheating in exams) is emotionally significant and can impact upon his treatment. Prevalent among patients with pronounced, even if compensated, narcissistic and sociopathic traits (Kernberg, 1984; Stone, 2009) such withholding can manifest through "silence" but can also exist under the mask of pseudo-cordial verbalisation. However, it should be remembered that relatively "intact" neurotic patients can also consciously withhold information (e.g., the price of a recently purchased house) out of anxiety and transference-based fears of shame, competitiveness, and hostility.

Enactive silence

The "deliberate withholding" mentioned above might be a way of avoiding personal shame, anticipated ridicule by the analyst, or behind-the-back gossip or mocking by real or imagined third parties (e.g., the analyst's colleagues or spouse with whom the analyst is assumed to share secrets). Until the time such motivation governs withholding, the practice falls under what Arlow (1961) has called "silences which serve primarily the function of defense" (p. 49). However, if the aim of deliberate withholding is to mislead the analyst, control him, and render him impotent, then the phenomenon belongs to the category of "silences which serve primarily the function of discharge" (p. 49).

In contemporary terminology, silences of the latter type constitute enactments. By becoming or remaining silent, the patient is putting something into action and, at the same time, pulling the analyst into a reactive or reciprocal response. Such silence may be used to cause a "reinstinctualization of the process of empathy" (ibid., p. 51) in the analyst. It might be a way of teasing and hurting the analyst. Hiding under the cloak of "verbal invisibility", a tenaciously silent patient might attack the analytic process, freeze its progress, "kill time", and paralyse the analyst's "work ego" (Olinick, Poland, Grigg & Granatir, 1973). The activation and discharge of primitive sadomasochism is difficult to miss under such circumstances.

While it is hardly possible to exhaustively list the relational scenarios that are played out through relentless—and, often motionless (with the patient lying absolutely still on the couch)—silences, common "messages" from such patients include: (i) "Please do not try to kill me; I am already dead", (ii) "I am going to make it impossible for you to do your work; you will feel as worthless as I felt growing up in my family", (iii) "I am not going to talk no matter how much you want me to; I will make you feel how I felt when my father would become silent for days upon the slightest infraction of rules on my part", and so on. In other words, enactments in the form of silence can reflect self-protection, important identifications, reversals of traumatic childhood scenarios, "attacks on linking" (Bion, 1958), and destructiveness towards the treatment process.

Instinctual discharge and enactment of identifications (e.g., with silently hostile parents) are, however, not the only factors in the aetiology of such silence. Superego dictates might also contribute to it. Arlow clearly states that:

> I do not wish to leave the impression that silence in the service of discharge is related exclusively to gratification of id-impulses. Clinical experiences abound to show that failure, suffering, and provocation in analytic situations may serve the self-punitive demands of the superego, and transference repetition may represent a persistent need to expiate guilt by using silence as a provocation of punishment. (1961, p. 51)

Symbolic silence

The contemporary eclipse of the "drive theory" perspective[3] should not make one overlook that what appears as silence might be a displaced, symbolic derivative of other instinctual aims. For instance, silence in obsessional neurotics is often a manifestation of anal erotism

(Ferenczi, 1916): mouth replaces the anus and words get equated with faeces under such circumstances. "Retaining words" become a vehicle of controlling a mother who insists upon proper toilet habits. Sharpe enlarged the scope of the drive-based aims that could be expressed via silence.

> When the ego stabilizes the achievement of body-control and it becomes automatic, the emotions of anger and pleasure which heretofore accompanied bodily discharges must be dealt with in other ways. At the same time as sphincter control over anus and urethra is being established, the child is acquiring the power of speech and so an avenue of "outerance" present from birth becomes of immense importance.
>
> First of all the discharge of feeling tension when this is no longer relieved by physical discharges can take place through speech. The activity of speaking is substituted for the physical activity now restricted at other openings of the body, while words themselves become the very substitutes for the bodily substances. (1940, p. 157)

Thus, silence can represent an open mouth waiting for the milk of the mother-analyst's voice, a tightly closed anus refusing to yield faeces for a pleading mother or a welcoming vagina ready to receive the father-analyst's "phallic" interpretations. However, such thinking has become sidelined in the current fervour of object relations, intersubjectivity, and an overall pallor of psychoanalytic interest in the body (Paniagua, 2004). Sharpe's perspective that silence might symbolise other bodily phenomena has lost its audience. Even less recognised is the fact that traffic moves in the opposite direction as well. In other words, other organs can be enlisted to express silence. Eyes are particularly important in this regard. Averting gaze and refusing to look at someone can be deployed as a form of not talking to them; this can have devastating effects upon the one who is thus shut out. A growing child, encountering such "visual silence" might find it hard to sustain self-esteem, and his capacity for object constancy might suffer (Abrams, 1991; Riess, 1978). Even during adulthood, being subject to such relational silence can be very disconcerting (Patsy Turrini, personal communication, February, 2012). The following poem of mine, titled *Silent Eyes*, attempts to capture the anguish-suffused experience.

Silent eyes, silent eyes.
I can't take them any more.
No. No. No more,
Silent eyes.

When all your doors say "no entry",
There is nothing I can claim.
When you turn your face away from me,
I die a thousand deaths of shame.

Silent eyes, silent eyes.
I can't take them any more.
No. No. No more,
Silent eyes.

When you mirror me no longer,
I can barely see my face.
On your love's dining table,
I can hardly find a place.

Silent eyes, silent eyes,
I can't take them any more.
No. No. No more,
Silent eyes.

Such dreadful turning-away of the object and the resulting "torture by separation" (Sartre, 1946, p. 8) bring to mind that silence can symbolise death. Wurmser's (2000) observation that the German word *Totschweigen* stands for "to kill by silence" is also pertinent here. Wurmser notes that such "soul blindness"—a sustained and profound insensitivity (including visual aversion) to someone's individuality—can lead to structural disintegration in the recipient. Within the clinical situation, a tenacious silence often transmits a sense of putrefaction and deadness. The patient seems to be "playing possum" and thus avoiding an imagined attack from the analyst while at the same time "killing" the analyst off.

Contemplative silence

A slowing down of perceptual and cognitive traffic as well as a certain "low keyedness"[4] of affect is essential for fresh insights to emerge from within (Ronningstam, 2006) and/or new information from outside to be metabolised. The associated stoppage of active speech falls under the rubric of "contemplative silence". The individual, in this state, is involved in a private and subliminal dialogue with his subjectively experienced inner objects (Mahler, Pine & Bergman, 1975; Winnicott, 1963) or turning attention inward to comprehend and catalogue what he has just heard or seen.

The pensive quietude that follows reading poetry, looking at a striking piece of art, and even upon hearing seriously bad national news is an illustration of "contemplative silence". In the context of our clinical work, such silence appears spontaneously and is followed by a meaningful revelation or enhancement of associations. Or it appears in response to the analyst's intervention.

> Some patients need some "silent time" to mull over, to contend with, to digest the new insight. This will be followed by confirmatory material if the interpretation is correct. It is a much more frequent occurrence, however, to find that patients will react with silence to an incorrect interpretation. In this situation, silence usually indicates the disappointment in not being understood. Usually such silences in response to interpretation are transient. Prolonged silence after an interpretation always means that the interpretation has been incorrect. (Greenson, 1961, pp. 82–83)

Clearly, the clinical situation is not the sole arena for contemplative silences to emerge. As stated above, appreciation of art and literature is regularly reliant on such quietness of mind. Rapt absorption in pondering over scientific and mathematical problems as well as seeming oblivion before a writer puts pen to paper are also instances of contemplative silence.[5] The "recess" a judge takes before giving his judgment in a court of law is also pertinent in this context.

Nowhere is "contemplative silence" more evident than in the state of mourning.[6] Withdrawal of cathexis from the external world and the need to shuffle the relational cards involving the lost objects lead to a certain quietness on the bereaved person's part. Feeling humbled by the awesome power of death, one loses faith—for a moment—in spoken words. Communion with the internal representations of the deceased, and the awareness of one's own mortality render one wary of platitudes. Attention turns towards the changed reality, and the gaping hole produced by the loss is covered over by silence.

Regenerative silence

Within psychoanalysis, the notion of an ego-replenishing quietude was first introduced by Winnicott (1963). According to him, genuine communication only arises when objects change over from being subjective to being objectively perceived. It is at this point that the two opposites of communication also appear. One is active or reactive not-communicating and the other "simple not-communicating" (p. 183). This is what I have termed "regenerative silence" here. In Winnicott's words:

> Simple not-communicating is like resting. It is a state in its own right, and it passes over into communicating, and reappears as naturally ... One should be able to make a positive statement of the healthy use of non-communication in the establishment of feeling real. (pp. 183–184)

Such not-communicating is seen by Winnicott to restore the vitality of true self which by its very nature is incommunicado and most worthy of preservation. His notions in this realm have been further developed by Khan (1983a, 1983b). In describing the sate of "lying fallow", Khan declared that this:

> ... is not one of inertia, listless vacancy or idle quietism of soul; nor is it a flight from harassed purposiveness and pragmatic action. *Lying fallow* is a transitional state of experience, a mode of being that is alerted quietude and receptive wakeful lambent consciousness ... We need to be somewhat idle and feel our way out of this benignly languid passive mood. If we are forced out of it, either by our own conscious or the environment, we feel irritable and grumpy. (pp. 183, 185, italics in the original)

Khan regards the experience of "lying fallow" to be "a nutrient of the ego" (p. 185) and important for the process of personalisation in the individual. Unlike Winnicott, he suggests that while silent inactivity is the most frequent pathway to such experience, it can also be reached by pictorial expression, as through doodling. Moreover, the experience, while deeply personal and private, can be facilitated by the silent companionship of someone—a spouse, friend, or even an unintrusive pet. This is "silence in the service of ego" (Shafii, 1973, p. 431) *par excellence*.

Blank silence

The consideration of diminished content and velocity of thought in the "lying fallow" state leads to the next logical step of total absence of activity in the mind: no verbally encoded thoughts, no visual images, no affective currents. To be sure, a proposal of this sort causes puzzlement and raises flags of scepticism. One wants to protest. Would not such a state be equivalent to "psychic death" (Guntrip, 1969) or betray a withdrawal from object cathexes that is of psychotic proportions? How could the mind become still to this extent, unless there was a "negative hallucination of thought" (Green, 1993) operative *in toto*? In other words, the theoretician amongst (and within) us might reluctantly concede that "blank silence" exists but only if he can declare it to be seriously pathological.

Such thinking can certainly explain a certain form of "blank silence", a "malignant" one, I suppose. However, there might be a benign type of "blank silence" also. Indeed, it was in this latter sense that Van der Heide first proposed the term. He regarded it as representing a blissful merger of the self and object, also seen in close proximity to sleep. Such silence usually occurs in response to a concise and correct transference interpretation.

> The patient falls into a silence of many minutes or lasting for the remainder of the session. His position on the couch is relaxed, often the habitual one of sleep; there is no sign of motor activity, speech has vanished and is not attempted. It looks like "time out". If the analyst succeeds in terminating the silence by urging verbalization (which rarely succeeds), he is told that thoughts were absent and there is no evidence of conscious withholding of thoughts or fantasy. If after a time the silence breaks spontaneously, the spoken thoughts appear distant from the content of the interpretation. Sometimes the patient ends the silence with a remark evidencing awareness of the analyst's thoughts or momentary affective state. (1961, p. 86)

In Van der Heide's view, "blank silence" serves the aims of primary identification and narcissism and, though peaceful, is a regressive phenomenon (see also Khan, 1983b). An opposite view is evident in Buddhism. Emphasising the potentially transcendent powers of silence, Buddhism declares that

True inner silence puts you in touch with the deeper dimensions of being and knowing—gnostic awareness and innate wisdom. Because it is impossible to express the inexpressible, the spiritual sound or song of silence is beyond words and concepts. Mere words are weak translations of what we really want to say. Inner silence and emptiness can help provide easier access to universal mystery and primordial being …. Silence is a threshold to the inner sanctum, the heart's sublime cave. Silence is the song of the heart, like love, a universal language, a natural melody open to anyone, even the tone-deaf or religiously challenged …. Inner solitude and "Noble Silence" is a way to empty, cleanse, heal, and renew the heart and mind. (Das, 1997, pp. 223–224, 226)

To be sure, there are echoes of "contemplative" and "regenerative" silences (see above) here. Or have we come full circle back to where we started this discussion on silence's typology, namely to "structural silence"? The equation of benign "blank silence" with "structural silence", however, overlooks that the former is achieved (and not given) and is associated with existential transcendence. As the attempted integration of Buddhism and psychoanalysis (Coltart, 1996; Epstein, 1995; Nichol, 2006; Rubin, 1996) evolves further, this remote corner of metapsychology might remain less unlit than it is now.

A sociocultural digression

A brief foray into the sociocultural matrices of silence might not be out of place at this point. Questions abound in this realm. Are some cultures (e.g., Japanese) more respecting of silence while others (e.g., North American) put more of a premium on verbalisation? Do socially taboo topics create different areas of silence in different cultures? Is there variability in the degree of cross-generational candour (and, hence, also of silence) from culture to culture? Can social class determine the strength or even existence of a voice? And so on.

While interdisciplinary studies search for answers to these (and often, related) questions, my digression into the cultural realm focuses upon five groups of people for whom silence (both literal and metaphorical) is an integral aspect of existence. I must concede that these somewhat arbitrarily constructed categories might represent, on a "macro level", corresponding but fragmented self-representations that lie at the core of all of us: (i) the voiceless, (ii) the oppressed, (iii) the dislocated, (iv) the complicit, and (v) the worshipper.

Silence of the voiceless

The well-known quip that history is written by winners gives expression to the sad truth that there exists in each era and each social system a group of individuals who lack a "voice". And, since what is given voice gets registered and can be recalled and what lacks articulation gets forgotten, the tale of the voiceless dissolves into oblivion. Children, the illiterate, and the very poor, ethnic groups whose identities have been crushed by genocide (e.g., Native Americans), and, till recently, women, "coloured" people, homosexuals, and those with physical disabilities, all belonged to this category. Not given the proper tools (e.g., education, access to information, respect for their minds, transportation, and accessibility) to construct a consciousness of will and personalisation, members of these groups can not (or, till recently, could not) evolve a linguistically-based canonical narrative of their existence. Spivak's (1988) pithy question, "Can the subaltern speak?", while raised in relation to "third world" women, can readily be addressed to all those who are/feel voiceless in today's world. Psychoanalysis can do little about this. However, by joining hands with anthropology, political science, history, and sociology, it might assist in information retrieval and construction of consciousness and "voice" in some such groups. Illustration of this is to be found in the recent works of Atwood (2007), Grenville (2007), Steel (2007), and San Roque (2007) that deal with the traumatic past of Australia and the rejuvenation of the Aboriginal mind and culture.

Silence of the oppressed

Distinct from the "voiceless" are the oppressed. They have a voice and know what they want to say and would savour the opportunity to do so. Yet fear of reprisal keeps their lips sealed. Adolescents dominated by tyrannically conservative parents, women battered by hateful men, spouses controlled by paranoid partners, and masses terrorised by totalitarian dictators, while dying to speak often contend with the speechlessness of living death. They have little recourse except to comply with the oligarchy of sadism. The history of Europe's colonial rule in Africa and Asia, slavery in the United States, apartheid in South Africa, and various other disenfranchising strictures in nations across the globe provide ample illustrations of the "silence of the oppressed". Underneath the overt surrender of voice lie resentment and bitterness, fantasies of rebellion and revenge, and hope for breaking the chains of psychosocial imprisonment.

In Fivush's (2010) terminology, these are not instances of "being silent"; these are illustrations of "being silenced". The former is mostly elective. The latter is imposed and signifies loss of personal power and esteem. The culturally dominant narrative (e.g., of the coloniser) silences societal experiences that do not fit its frame. This can take the form of not letting people speak and depriving them of the right to assembly or by refusing to believe their version of social reality. Such imposed silence can hamper the sharing of the present with the younger generation and preclude socially mediated interpretations of the past (Fivush, 2001; Fivush & Nelson, 2004).

Silence of the dislocated

The immigrant and the exile are also "silent" in certain ways. Encountering unfamiliar landscapes, climate, vegetation, and architecture often results in subtle but important perceptual disturbances of the ego (Akhtar, 1999, 2011; Grinberg & Grinberg, 1989). The individual no longer experiences a seamless fusion with the ecological surround or a painless demarcation from it. He finds insufficient opportunity to cross and recross without challenge "the transitional area between synaesthesia and sensory compartmentalisation" (Kafka, 1989, p. 47). The freedom to fuse and separate different modalities is no longer available to him. This perceptual liberty underlies the capacity to create and enjoy metaphor. The fresh immigrant, however, lacks opportunities to move freely between the self-abandonment of rapture and the alertness of task-orientation, between perceiving the figure and ground separately sometimes and together at other times, and between the dreamy conflation of sensory modalities and a hyper-realistic separation of them. Poetry of communication escapes him. Literalness is his prison.

Being a stranger to local quips and witticisms, the immigrant appears awkwardly "silent". He does not comprehend the poems and jokes of his new nation. His "mutism" is even more marked when it comes to matters of history; not having been properly schooled in the nation's history and not having lived through important events in the country of adoption, he finds little to say about them. Finally, there is the sad infrequency with which he can use his mother tongue, especially during the work day. The pain of such silence is eloquently described by Kristeva (1988, p. 20):

> Not to speak your own mother tongue. To live with sounds, logics, that are separated from the nocturnal memory of the body, from the sweet-sour sleep of childhood. To carry within yourself like a secret crypt or like a handicapped child—loved and useless—that language of once-upon-a-time that fades and won't make up its mind to leave you ever. You learn to use another instrument, like expressing yourself in algebra or on the violin. You can become a virtuoso in this new artifice that provides you with a new body, just as false, sublimated—some would say sublime. You have the impression that the new language is your resurrection: a new skin, a new sex. But the illusion is torn apart when you listen to yourself—on a recorded tape, for example—and the melody of your own voice comes back to you in a bizarre way, from nowhere, closer to the grumble of the past than to the [linguistic] code of today .... Thus, between two languages, your element is silence. (Cited in Amati-Mehler, Argentieri & Canestri, 1993, pp. 264–265)

All in all, immigration and exile result in a silence that involves the pre-migration core of the self and that is both literal and metaphorical in nature.

Silence of the complicit

On both individual and group levels, complicity with crimes and cruelties by others is often manifest via the bystanders' silence. Shengold's (1989) descriptions of "soul murder" (i.e., the malevolent erasure of someone's humanity, identity, and perceptual clarity) of a child by the parent often include the fact that the other parent watched the violation silently, without making any effort to stop what was going on. The sexual abuse literature is also replete with the deleterious impact of the "silent parent's" (Escoll, 1999) complicity upon the abused child. One parent defiles the child's body and the other averts his or her gaze and is thus an accomplice to the crime. Similar phenomena are evident on a group level. The silence of a nation's majority when a minority is being abused can be devastating to the latter. And, when the world's nations (or, at least some of them) fail to recognise genocides that have occurred or are occurring, the deafening silence can rupture the eardrums of mankind.

Less sinister though hardly forthright are the silences that members of cults, gangs, secret societies, and, regrettably, at times, the police force maintain as an act of loyalty to their respective organisations. The most well-known example is *omerta* or the popular code of honour common in areas of southern Italy (and among some Italian-Americans), which involves a categorical prohibition of cooperation with state authorities or reliance on its services. *Omerta* is essentially a code of silence that seals lips of men even in their own defence and even when the accused are innocent of the crime. Its purpose is to sustain group solidarity.[7]

Silence of the worshipper

In marked contrast to "silence of complicity" is "silence of the worshipper". Here, the individual intentionally detaches himself from the plebeian pressures of external reality and turns inwards in search of the sacred and the reverential. The self's focus shifts from the psychic representations of important others to a subdued dialogue with the "god representation" (Meissner, 1984, 2001; Rizzutto, 1979, 1996, 2001); this is a partly conscious and partly unconscious inner structure that is evolved by all children over the course of their development. Relationship with both parents contributes to the formation of this internal image. Dialogue with it revolves around conflicts over desire, shame, and guilt, reward and punishment, and the more complex matters of the meaning of life and death, origins of this universe, and what happens to living beings after they die. As one approaches this realm, a sense of mystery, awe, and humility descends upon one's existence (Ostow, 2001). Written texts and scriptures of organised religions can bring one up to this point but the journey from here onwards is traversed in silence. The emphasis upon such quietude in Buddhism has already been cited. Other religions, too, encourage the muting of a separated voice; places of worship are designed to inspire awe, mobilise humility, and stir up merger fantasies. Meditative practices in almost all religions (e.g., Judaism's solemn *Shabat*, Hinduism's *vipaasna*, Sufism's moments of *fana*, and Carmelite nuns' vows of cloistered silence) rely upon wordless encounter with the divine.

For the believer, this is a matter of mysticism and transcendence. For the psychoanalytic sceptic, however, it reflects a bypass of secondary process and an illusory re-creation of primary narcissism: objectless, suffused with "oceanic feeling" (Roland, cited in Freud, 1930a), and omnipotent. A compromise position might be that the experience is more than mere reaching back to the fused "all-good" self-object representation of infancy; it synthesises the personal with the cultural, and the ontogenetic with the iconic integrity distilled by generations. "If this is partial regression, it is a regression which, in retracing firmly established pathways, returns to the present amplified and clarified" (Erikson, 1958, p. 264).

Back to the clinical realm

While there are overlaps between them, for the purposes of didactic clarity, it might be better to consider the patient's silences, the analyst's silences, and their simultaneous silence separately.[8] Such nosological categorisation is by no means intended to endorse "one person psychology" over "two person psychology" and to deny that psychic phenomena can often not be understood in isolation from their interpersonal matrix. Much in the spirit of Dunn's (1995) sophisticated assessment of intersubjectivity, my perspective regards the positivistic tradition of the classical ego-psychology and the postmodern relational approaches to psychoanalysis (Mitchell, 1988, 1993; Ogden, 1986, 1994; Stolorow & Atwood, 1978) as coexistent and mutually additive, not contradictory and opposed to each other. Thus the compartmentalisation of silence in the clinical hour into those of the patient, those of the analyst, and those resulting from both parties being simultaneously quiet, needs to be viewed as only relative. Each of the three contains tributaries from the other two. That said, let us now turn to examining such silences in some detail.

Patient's silence

Like any other behaviour or communication on his or her part, the patient's silence is multiply-determined. It can serve defensive or discharge functions and can deplete the ego by banishing of useful psychic content into the unconscious, or replenish the ego by permitting quiet preconscious synthesis of fresh insights. It can represent deliberate withholding, unconscious resistance, a form of communication, an enactment of fantasy, attack upon the analytic setting ("killing time"), or merely a moment of contemplation.[9] As a result, no set rules can be laid down for dealing with patients' silences. Indeed, Arlow (1961) has reminded us that "nothing can replace the sensitivity of the therapist or his empathic response to the unfolding concatenation of influences at any moment in the transference" (p. 53). And yet, keeping the following points in mind, while faced with a patient's silence, can be helpful.

- Silence serves many purposes and resistance is only one of them (Arlow, 1961; Blos, 1972).
- Silence follows or precedes something emotionally significant.
- Silence can be spontaneous or in response to the analyst's intervention.
- Silence can be communicative; its timing and affective "tone" can convey a lot that is meaningful (Reik, 1948). In Sabbadini's (1992) words, "Behind all silence there is an unconscious fantasy which the silence—like the dream or the symptom—both conceals and expresses at the same time" (pp. 28–29).
- Silence is often accompanied by postural change, gestures, and other sounds including sobs, sighs, grunts; paying attention to these can reveal useful information to the analyst (Greenson, 1961; McLaughlin, 1987, 1992).
- Silence does not always impede and speaking does not always facilitate the aims of analysis.[10]
- Silence almost invariably has transference meanings and therefore a careful scrutiny of the countertransference experience is of great help in discerning what is going on in the clinical process.

It is in the setting of such a backdrop that I offer the following two clinical vignettes that demonstrate the complex interactions between drive and discharge, the patient's own agenda and relational triggers in the here-and-now, transference and countertransference, and ultimately between affirmative and interpretive interventions.

Clinical vignette 1

Mary Robinson,[11] a schizoid woman in the first year of her brittle and tenuous analysis, begins a session by a prolonged silence. After waiting it out some, since I am used to her halting manner, I bring her attention to the difficulty she seems to be experiencing in beginning to talk. Encountering further silence, I venture, "Perhaps there is some concern, some anxiety that is making it difficult for you to reveal what you are thinking and feeling." Mary remains quiet for another few minutes. Then, in a pained voice, she says, "Why can't you understand me without my speaking? You are an analyst. You should be able to understand what I am feeling, what I am wanting and needing from you at this time." She pauses. I remain quiet. She adds, "It hurts my feelings when you want me to speak so that you can understand me. See, when I was little I had to teach my mother—at least, I tried to—how to be my mother. Then I had to teach my father how to be my father. And, now I have to speak here so that you can understand me. That's like my teaching you how to be an analyst. It hurts my feelings. It really does, this whole thing."

While she is not vengeful, her plaintive and hurt voice makes me feel I have burdened her. By encouraging verbalisation, I have imposed my agenda. Soon, however, I see the idealising aspect of her desire. I should omnisciently discern her inner world and she, having arrived at the Mecca of depth psychology, should be healed with little further effort on her part. I begin to feel sceptical. What is all this a defence against? Does the desire to keep me fixed in an idealised healer role help her ward off hate towards me for my seeming unhelpful (allegedly, like her parents)? Is this god-like view of me a shield to deflect her erotic and non-erotic feelings about my body, which is after all only about two feet from her? With these thoughts, an intervention begins to formulate in my mind. I will, in some fashion, bring her attention to the defensive aims in her statement.

However, I decide to give myself just another moment or two to think this out further. Now it occurs to me that while my line of thinking is plausible, it involves a rather swift bypass of the patient's overt material. Maybe there is something to what she is saying. Maybe her feeling hurt by my first intervention was not simply a response to a frustrated transference wish by an understandable reaction to the deprivation of a healthy ego need. After all, aren't there certain human relationships (e.g., between infant and mother, between two naked lovers under a sheet, between a religious mendicant and his or her spiritual guide, between two friends driving for a long while on a highway, etc.) where words are not essential for communication? Clearly, this patient did not have enough such ego-strengthening experiences during childhood and is not having enough such experiences in her adult life. To be sure, we should work at her resolving the intrapsychic hurdles in her path to be more satisfied in this regard, but what about this very moment when she seems to be in need of such an experience? Is there a point in depriving her? Should my follow-up intervention not indicate that I respect her need to be understood in her silence and that I did indeed burden her by encouraging her to talk? Should I interpret the idealising, defensive, and potentially paranoid aspect of her comments? Or should I empathise with her hurt, and discern and acknowledge the healthy, developmentally valid aspect of her ego need? Arriving at this conceptual fork, I decide to take the affirmative route and renounce the sceptical–interpretive possibilities for the moment.

In doing so, I let Loewenstein's (1961) reminder that silence, in analysis as well as outside it, is at times a necessary mode of object relationship become my guide. I also found support in Arlow's (1961) observation that in prolonged and deep human relationships, "It is possible for the verbalized aspects of communication to be reduced to a minimum, to representation by small signals, and finally, to expression by silences" (p. 50). Indeed, Nacht (1964) asserts that even though an unconscious drive towards fusion might underlie the patient's need to express himself by silence, its gratification is often a necessary condition for the progress of analytic work.

Clinical vignette 2

In the throes of a regressive transference, Jill Schwartz entered my office enraged and waving a finger. Approaching the couch, she said, "I have a lot on my mind today and I want to do all the talking. I don't want you to speak even a single word!" A little taken aback, I mumbled, "Okay." Jill shouted, "I said, 'not one word' and you have already fucked up this session!" Now sitting on my chair behind her, I was rattled. "Did I do wrong by speaking at all?" I asked myself. As she lay on the couch, angrily silent and stiff, I started to think. Perhaps she is so inconsolable today, so intent upon forcing me into the role of a depriving person, that she found a way to see even the gratification of her desire as its frustration. I was, however, not entirely satisfied with this explanation and therefore decided to wait, and think further. It then occurred to me that maybe she was rightly angered by my saying 'Okay'. In my agreeing to let her have omnipotent control over me, I had asserted my will and thus paradoxically deprived her of the omnipotence she seemed to need. I was about to make an interpretation along these lines, when it occurred to me that by sharing this understanding, I would be repeating my mistake: making my autonomous psychic function-ing too obvious. As a result, I decided to only say, "I am sorry," and left the remaining thought unspoken. Jill relaxed and the tension in the room began to lessen. After ten minutes of further silence, she said, "Well, this session has been messed up. I had so many things to say." After a further pause, she said, "Among the various things on my mind …" and thus the session gradually "started". By the time we ended, things were going pretty smoothly.

In presenting this second vignette, I am trying to make three points. The *first* point is that by apologising to the patient, I was acknowledg-ing that I had failed her by not understanding that she needed to have no boundaries, as it were, between us at all; she was the kind of patient (at least at that moment) who "needs to be allowed to establish a pro-visional omnipotence over the analyst" (Casement, 1991, p. 277). The *second* point is that although my patient and I both remained silent for some ten to fifteen minutes (after the initial exchange in the ses-sion), our silences belonged to each of us separately. Her silence repre-sented a hurt and angry withdrawal. Mine started with not knowing what to say or do but, as the clock ticked by, turned into an "inter-pretive action" (Ogden, 1994). It is as if, by remaining silent, I was saying to her: "I understand that you have felt hurt by me and disap-pointed in me. As a result, you are trying to hold on to yourself and need some recuperative time before taking what seems to you the risk of relating to me," Both my patient and I were silent but we were silent separately, so to speak. The *third* point pertains to the fact that upon hearing the presentation of this vignette at a conference, some analytic colleagues in the audience questioned my not asking the patient what she had been thinking about during the long silence before she resumed talking. These clinicians felt that I had missed some very important data by lack of investigation. While seeing their point and having a certain sympathy with such a perspective, I held—and still hold—a different view of the situation. I believe that "not analysing" or letting go of that long silence was preferable because to do otherwise would (i) betray analytic greed, (ii) risk pathologising an introgenic event, and (iii) further deprive the patient of the omnipotence that she so desperately needed. In Arlow's words, my patient's tenacious refusal to speak constituted one of

> those silences which must be respected, silences which represent a period during which the patient struggles to maintain control over his feelings or to re-establish a sense of self-esteem after some recollection by the patient or some intervention by the therapist which may have wrought violence to the patient's narcissism. (1961, p. 54)

Technique might differ with patients who are resolutely silent on their own. Some of them do not speak for the entire hour and often continue to do so session after session. This usually happens in the setting of severe obsessional and schizoid character pathology. Bound to stir up strong countertransference reactions, such silences warrant an admixture of affirmative and "holding" (Winnicott, 1960b) and interpretive and limit-setting (Kernberg, 1984) measures. Encouraging, and educative remarks constitute one end of such an interventional continuum and having the patient sit up and "converting psychoanalysis into psychotherapy" (Akhtar, 2009, pp. 57–58) forms the other end. The area between these extremes is replete with technical challenges. The clinical approach of the British independent tradition (Balint, 1968; Coltart, 1993; Winnicott, 1963, 1965) recommends a long waiting period as the patient remains silent and motionless. The idea is to allow the patient for a sufficient length of time the security of being unquestioned and the support of a relational structure that enables him to spontaneously reveal his deepest concerns.[12] Premature rupture of such silence by interpretations is risky. In Winnicott's words,

> If we wait, we become objectively perceived in the patient's own
> time, but if we fail to behave in a way that is facilitating the patient's
> analytic process (which is the equivalent of the infant's and the
> child's maturational process), we certainly become "not me" for
> the patient, and then we know too much, and we are dangerous.
> Because we are too nearly in communication with the central, still
> and silent of the patient's ego organization. (1963, p. 189)

In contrast to this approach is the Kleinian and neo-Kleinian strategy.
Talking of a patient with psychotic vulnerability, Klein (1955) declared
that "I found from the first hour onwards that I must not allow the
patient to remain silent for any length of time. I felt that his silence
implied danger, and in every circumstance I interpreted his suspicions
of me" (p. 136). Kernberg, Selzer, Koenigsberg, Carr & Appelbaum also
recommend a more active technique in dealing with protracted silences.
They believe that

> a wait-and-see attitude to the patient's refusal to speak is a dan-
> gerous therapeutic posture for several reasons: it supports the
> patient's omnipotent view of having the right to exercise unbridled
> aggression; it fosters the therapist's reaching a point where he or
> she can no longer contain angry frustration; it collaborates with the
> patient's devaluation of the therapist by suggesting that both of
> them sanction a do-nothing attitude. (1989, p. 172)

Kernberg and colleagues recommend confronting the patient with the
contradiction between coming regularly to seek help and not speaking, and his omnipotent attitude towards time which permits him to
go on with one useless session after another. They recommend that the
therapist evolve a tentative hypothesis about the nature of the difficulty interfering with the patient's speaking and communicate it to the
patient in a forthright manner.[13]

The two approaches outlined above reflect what Strenger (1989)
has termed the "romantic" and "classic" visions of psychoanalysis. Most practising clinicians intuitively attempt to strike their own
variety of balance between these extreme positions. It is also conceivable that protracted silences of schizoid patients respond better
to the Winnicottian approach, silences of borderline patients to the
Kernbergian approach, and silences of obsessional patients to an

"informed oscillation" (Akhtar, 2000) between these two technical strategies. In the end, though, the choice of which perspective to address the silence from depends on the analyst's empathic evaluation of its inherent transference communication and intuitive evaluation of the patient's capacity to understand and utilise the intervention. Vigilance towards the countertransference experience is extremely important in such situations. Here it should be noted that the analyst's tolerance of patients' silences tends to vary with his or her character structure. Working through of narcissism and manic defences greatly helps. Growing older and having raised children might also enhance the analyst's capacity to bear patients' silences, with their potential for coming across as unrelatedness. The analyst's cultural background might also play a role. With unusual candour, Ronningstam addresses this issue.

> I grew up in a Protestant farming village in northern Sweden, close to the Arctic Circle, on the same latitude as northern Alaska, middle Greenland and northern Siberia. The Gulf Stream contributed to a relatively warm climate with marked contrasts between the seasons. At the winter solstice, the sun barely reached over the horizon, and at midsummer it barely reached under the horizon providing 24-hour daylight. Although I was fortunate to grow up in a community where people did speak and communicate, still, silence was a predominant phenomenon. Some silences were restful and thoughtful, and words were not necessary. Other silences were empty because words were missing, especially for conveying feelings. Still other silences could be described by a truism, i.e., "speech is silver but silence is gold". But silence could also represent distancing and/or elimination of threatening, painful or hateful matters and experiences. People embedded their losses, failures or scandals in silence. They treated their enemies with silence, and managed overwhelming conflicts and threats in silence. They waited in silence, grieved in silence, and rejoiced or prided themselves in silence. In anthropological terms, I have a high culturally determined tolerance for silence and, in psychoanalytic terms, silence is to a high degree ego-syntonic to me. (2006, p. 1287)

Before bringing this section on patients' silences to a close, a matter of daily clinical occurrence must be addressed. This pertains to pauses in the patient's communication. Such momentary silences vary greatly in nature and warrant different responses from the analyst. A pause reflecting "contemplative silence" in which the patient is receiving information from within or reflecting upon what the analyst has just said needs to be left undisturbed. A pause that appears immediately after a conjunction (e.g., "… and", "… or"), and followed by a change of topic betrays anxiety with continuing the line of original thought. This needs to be pointed out. For instance, when a patient says, "I want to sell my house and …", pauses for a few seconds and then goes on to speak of something else, the analyst might bring the patient's attention to having left the sentence unfinished. The analyst might even ask him to fill in the blank that followed "and …". In essence, a pause that aborts a thought midway is defensive in nature. In contrast is a pause that acts like a comma, following a finished clause, and leads to continuation of that thought. Here are two examples. A highly promiscuous divorced narcissistic man said, "In light of my hunger for women, it is good that I did not marry," paused, and then added, "I mean a second time" (betraying that he was not truly married even the first time). And a depressed young woman said, "Sometimes I think of committing suicide," paused, and then added, "Well, not really." Such silences are not defensive; words that follow them are defensive. As a result, technical intervention directed at them might note how difficult it became for the patient to contemplate what he or she had just revealed. To reiterate, pauses of contemplative type need no intervention, pauses of abortive type need confrontation, and pauses followed by a corrective addition to the original thought need empathic underscoring of the emotional significance of that thought.

Analyst's silence

Under ordinary circumstances, "The silence of an empathic, attentive, listening analyst helps the patient to tolerate the abstinence created by and necessary for the analytic process" (Zeligs, 1961, p. 19). The analyst's silence acts like a vase into which the patient can pour the liquid of free association. Paradoxically, the analyst's silence also grants the patient the right to remain quiet if he or she is unable to speak. Regardless of whether it encourages verbalisation or permits silence on the patient's part, the analyst's silence becomes a "container" (Bion, 1962b) that facilitates the processing of what is unmentalised and inchoate into a coherent narrative located within the matrix of ontogenetic and transference experience.

Clinical vignette 3

Rebecca Cohen, twenty-six-year-old daughter of a Holocaust survivor father, was in analysis with me. The course of early treatment was filled with anxiety-laden fantasies about her father's experience in the Nazi concentration camp. Dreaded scenarios of ethnic hatred and violence preoccupied Rebecca and this readily spread to the transference. She feared and hated me, regarded me as a Jew-hating Muslim or Arab, and suspected that I supported anti-Israeli violence by Palestinians. Projections of her own trans-generationally given post-traumatic Jew-Nazi split of the self were constantly active in her relatedness with me. One day, I was hated and viciously attacked. Next day, I was deeply feared.

During one session while talking of the Holocaust, she suddenly jumped up from the couch and ran to the corner of the office that was farthest from me, trembling and obviously shaken by something she had just experienced internally. Rebecca stood there crying. I remained silent. Then she found a box of tissues on the desk nearby, cleaned her face and began to look a bit composed. I did not say anything and waited patiently for things to unfold. Rebecca jumped up, sat on my desk, and asked me if I knew what had happened. I shook my head, telling her that I did not. She then revealed that she had felt that I was going to take out a knife and stab her while she was on the couch and that's why she had to get away from me. As she was narrating this, I noted that she had become much calmer. I remained quiet. Rebecca went on to say, "You know, I have never seen your office from this end. It looks so strange … you know, what it looks like … it looks so still. Everything is unmoved, quiet. It is like a dust cover jacket of a best-seller murder mystery. And you know what, sometimes when you read the whole book, you find out that all the clues were already shown in the photograph on the cover of the book. Yes, your office, from this side, looks like a photograph of just that sort, with all the clues intact." Now I spoke. I said, "And, I guess I would be the corpse in this murder scene." Rebecca smiled, stretched her arms, and aiming her clasped hands at me, made a noise indicating that she was shooting me with a gun. I responded by saying "You know what, a little while ago you thought that I was going to kill you and now that you have taken some distance from that position, you find yourself killing me. Look, this murder and murderer are both parts of your own self and, for the work we have mutually undertaken, it is my hope that we hold on to both these views and see how they are related to each other, where they came from, and what purposes do they serve." Rebecca got off the desk, walked back to the couch, and lay down. The session continued in the "usual" way.

This clinical exchange illustrates a number of interventions, including the interpretation of splitting and projective identification. However, what I wish to emphasise here is how my unperturbed and non-intrusive stance facilitated the unfolding of the clinical material. My verbal interventions were important but these became possible only because of the material that became available due to my remaining silent. Such beneficial effects of the analyst's silence should not lead us to overlook the instances where the consequences are just the opposite. It is therefore important to remember that:

- The analyst's silence is not always experienced by the patient as kind and helpful. The ideal state of being an "unobtrusive analyst" (Balint, 1968) does not necessarily imply remaining quiet.
- The analyst's silence can be due to countertransference feelings of boredom, indifference, or hostility and as such can hurt the patient.
- The analyst's silence can be a retaliatory response to the patient's silence and can contribute to a non-verbal stalemate in analysis (Glover, 1955).
- The analyst's silence, if prolonged, can be especially painful for patients with early childhood deprivations and the resulting attitude of oral fixation. Since they are likely to introject both the words and silences of the analyst (Zeligs, 1961), excessive internalisation of the latter sort can add to their own emptiness.[14] Mitrani (2001) has reported in detail upon a patient who experienced her silences as "the dangerous unknown" (p. 17) and "needed to hear my [Mitrani's] voice in order to allay her fears that I had deserted her" (p. 17). Long before Mitrani's contribution, Boyer (1980) and Volkan (1987) had reported an early "noisy phase" when the analyst grunts more than usual to assure his sicker patients of his continued involvement.
- The analyst's silence, if excessive, can have the effect of rendering his words too emotionally charged for the patient. "A silent analyst sets the stage for an analysis in which suggestion comes to play a highly

important role …. Excessive silence on the part of the analyst may achieve the opposite of what he may hope to achieve by what he calls analytic neutrality" (Brockbank, 1970, p. 459).

- The analyst's silence, in sum, has the potential of evoking varied ego states and drive tensions in the patient. A silence felt as libidinous can stir up fantasies of fusion and sex while one experienced as hostile can lead to feelings of rejection or retaliation. Silence as a symbol of death may evoke feelings of destructiveness and guilt on the part of the patient, with the analyst becoming the damaged object (Kreuzer-Haustein, 1994).

When all is said and done, matters boil down to this. The analyst's silence can both help and harm the analytic process. An improperly timed and countertransferentially motivated silence can disturb the process (as can an injudicious verbal intervention). A tactful silence, in contrast, can nudge the process further along (as can an appropriate verbal intervention). What this tells us is that the analyst's silence works pretty much as do his words. However, because of their "invisibility", misuses of and mistakes via silence are less often noted in practice and infrequently published in literature.

Simultaneous silence

There are moments and, at times, long stretches of time when both the analyst and the analysand are quiet. Broadly speaking such silences can be seen as belonging to two distinct categories. The first or *concurrent silence* occurs when an angry non-verbal stalemate develops within the dyad. The patient feels bitter and mistrustful and stops talking. The analyst, stung by feeling misunderstood, does not know what to say or, worse, punitively retaliates by remaining silent. The two parties though silent simultaneously seem to be following different agendas. A more benign version of such "separate" silences is when a patient seems to be thinking about what the analyst has said and the latter waits quietly. Here, too, the two parties are on somewhat different tracks. These and other similar silences of both parties when each is involved in his or her individual mental activity (see, for instance, clinical vignette 2 above) can be collectively termed "concurrent silences".

In contrast is *mutual silence* in the analytic hour which connotes a state of wordless communion between the two parties in the clinical dyad. They feel peaceful, are attuned to each other, but have little need to speak (Elson, 2001). The following vignette illustrates this phenomenon.

Clinical vignette 4

> Marcy Schectman begins the last session of her nearly ten-year-long analysis by saying that on her way to my office, she felt as if she were coming to a funeral. She describes her experience of there being an air of finality, solemnity, and loss to the afternoon. As I remain silent, Marcy goes on to recount her experiences at a couple of funerals she has attended. She sobs. I too feel sad, but do not say anything. Gradually, her associations shift to her getting a doctorate soon and then to graduation dinners, commencement ceremonies, etc. She begins to be animated. Soon, however, she catches herself and observes that this talk of happy endings (graduations) is defensive against her sadness (funerals). Significantly, she adds that while this might be the case, the two sides most likely represent the two sides of her feelings regarding parting from me for good: "happy and sad, sad and happy". I now say, "Yes, it does seem like that," and, after a momentary pause, add "But you know, all well-timed funerals are graduations of a sort and all graduations contain funeral-like elements." Marcy nods in agreement. She remains silent and so do I for the next couple of minutes. The sense of our being together in each other's apartness is evident as the end of the session approaches.

Clearly "our" silence during these last few minutes of her analysis can be viewed as multiply-determined. It is possible to view our not speaking as refusing to let the separating impact of words (sounds and voice) rob us of an illusory merger before we part for good in actuality. Also discernible is a last-ditch effort to capture the "dual unity" (Mahler, Pine & Bergman, 1975) or the "hallucinatory or delusional somatopsychic omnipotent fusion with the representation of the mother and, in particular, the delusion of a common boundary between two separate individuals" (p. 45). However, to the extent that our silence is not only mutual but also includes the echoes of highly individual personal experiences, the phenomenon comes close to what Kafka (1989) has termed the "primary paradox of individuation". According to him, a healthy mother-child symbiosis, by its very nature, permits the child to grow and step away from its mother. "Primary paradox of individuation" implies that "love and mutual acceptance of separateness have become subjectively equivalent" (p. 33).

Concluding remarks

In this chapter, I have addressed the multifaceted phenomenon of silence and described eight types of silence: (i) structural silence; (ii) silence due to the lack of mentalisation; (iii) silence due to conflict; (iv) silence as enactment; (v) symbolic silence; (vi) contemplative silence; (vii) regenerative silence, and (viii) blank silence. I have placed silence on an equal footing with speaking—especially as these occur in the psychoanalytic setting—by emphasising that both possess the ability to serve similar aims. Both can hide and both can express psychic contents. Both can defend against drive-related pressures and both can help discharge such tensions. Both can convey transference and both can become vehicles of enactment. Both can induce and evoke countertransference feelings. Both can be responded to appropriately or inappropriately by the patient. Both can facilitate or impede the progress of the analytic process. Through all this and more, both silence and verbalisation become integral to our clinical enterprise. At this point, I have made a brief digression into the socio-cultural realm and commented upon the silences of (i) the voiceless, (ii) the oppressed, (iii) the dislocated, (iv) the complicit, and (v) the worshipper. I have then returned to the clinical arena and distinguished the aims and consequences of the patient's silence and the analyst's silences. In addition to delineating the technical principles involving such silences of short and long duration, I have described the phenomenon of "mutual silence" in the clinical hour and elucidated its ontogenetic as well as "anagogic" (Silberer, 1914) foundations.

Now, I wish to conclude by noting some questions that have remained unaddressed in this discourse. These include the following. Does gender play a role in the capacity for expressing oneself through silence or in bearing others' silences? Are there developmental phases where silence, at least in regard to spoken language, is inevitable (e.g., early infancy) or preferred (e.g., old age)? Is silence (around oneself or in parts of oneself) conducive to creative work? Is silence an integral component of that ubiquitous human process called mourning and that elusive character attribute called "dignity"? To be sure, future contributions might provide answers to such questions but we must leave the possibility open for some of those answers to come without the veil of words. We must allow our knowledge to be enriched by a new manuscript of silence.

Notes

1. In light of this, it is striking to note that "silence" is not listed in the index of the *Standard Edition* of Freud's writings and is also missing from Fenichel's (1945) encyclopedic compendium of early psychoanalytic literature. The situation has changed dramatically, though, and a recent search on PEP Web yielded eighty papers with "silence" in their titles.
2. Talking of the generally alexithymic psychosomatic patients, Baranger and Baranger (2009) speak of interventions that "supply words to describe experiences that never had any. In this type of interpretation, the analyst proceeds *per via di porre* and not only *per via di levare*, as Freud (1905) demanded in referring to neurotics" (p. 102).
3. Pine (1988, 1997) continues to remind us, however, that the heuristic corpus of psychoanalysis consists of four psychologies: drive psychology, ego psychology, object relations psychology, and self psychology. They overlap but each adds something new to the understanding of development, psychopathology, and technique.
4. "Low keyedness" is a term originated by Mahler, Pine, and Bergman (1975) to describe a specific affectomotor state seen in toddlers when separated from their mothers. This state is characterised by slowing down of motility, diminution of interest in the external world, and shifting of attention towards inner experience. All this rapidly disappears upon mother's return. According to the authors, this state reflects the child's effort to inwardly hold on to an ideal state of the self, especially as it was experienced in a pleasant closeness with the mother.
5. The well-known psychoanalyst-philosopher, Allen Wheelis, told me that he often sits quietly for hours before beginning to write (personal communication, January 2008).
6. Note in this connection the ritual "moment of silence" observed in honour of the deceased. Its purpose is to enforce—temporarily at least—respectful attention upon the memories of the departed one.
7. It might seem strange to leap from the Sicilian *omerta* to the silence that we psychoanalysts maintain about transgressions within our own profession. We remain strangely silent in the face of boundary violations by our prominent colleagues. We say little as Stekel fabricates clinical material (Bos & Groenendijk, 2006), Khan merrily declares himself to be a prince (Hopkins, 2006), and Kohut reports on the two analyses of Mr Z. who in fact was most likely Kohut himself and there had been no second analysis (Giovacchini, 2000; Strozier, 2004). Even more

striking is the lack of discourse on the implications of Freud's signing "Dr Sigm Freud u frau" (German for Dr Sigmund Freud and *wife*" when he checked into a hotel in Maloja, Switzerland, on August 13, 1898 with his *wife's sister*, Minna Bernays (Blumenthal, 2006).

8. The technical considerations outlined here refer to adult patients only. Work with children and adolescents might pose different challenges, provide different opportunities, and carry different nuances of technique. However, not having the pertinent clinical experience, I am not qualified to comment upon this realm of clinical psychoanalysis.

9. My focus here is on psychodynamic dimensions of the phenomenon and does not involve medical-psychiatric syndromes associated with silence and mutism. The reader interested in the latter might want to look up Akhtar and Buckman (1977) for the differential diagnosis of mutism in adult patients, Kolvin and Fundudis (1981), Wong (2010), and Roberts (2002) for the multifaceted problem of elective mutism in children.

10. That incessant talking, without a pause for self-reflection or space for the analyst to intervene, can act as a resistance has been recognised from the earliest days of psychoanalysis (Ferenczi, 1915). More recently, Akhtar (2007) has delineated guidelines for the analyst's interrupting such flow of patients' speech and Baranger and Baranger (2009) have mentioned "misleading logorrhea" (p. 181) as a reflection of difficulty in genuine free association.

11. The names given to this patient and to all others that follow are fictitious.

12. See also Modell's (1975) notion of the "cocoon phase" of transference in narcissistic personalities.

13. Such "one-sided" understanding is inevitably based upon the countertransference experience though it might have been shaped by the patient's projective identifications. Earlier analysts (e.g., Loomie, 1961) had considered the use of an analyst's own associations in remarks to the patient as particularly bold. Contemporary psychoanalysts, especially those with a relational bent, however, more readily support this sort of intervention.

14. The deleterious impact of the analyst's silence is even more evident in the setting of supervision where careful listening to the candidate's presentation should be sprinkled with questions, attempts at clarification, observations, empathic remarks, and, occasionally, suggestions for alternative ways of understanding and intervening. Some supervisors, however, act as caricatures of a "classical" analyst, and I have heard of one who would remain totally silent throughout the supervisory hour. Needless to say that this greatly puzzled and traumatised the young trainee.

CHAPTER THREE

Listening to actions

"The patient does not remember anything of what he has forgotten and repressed, but acts it out. He reproduces it not as a memory but as an action."

—Sigmund Freud (1914g, p. 150)

The preceding chapters have demonstrated that patients' associations, as well as their silences, are our important allies in unmasking (or reconstructing) the unconscious narratives that contribute to their anachronistic suffering. This background prepares us to address the communicative value of the patients' behaviour. Let me hasten to add that I am not referring to patients' actions in their "real" lives. My focus is upon patients' behaviour *within* the clinical situation and even more so upon the analyst's ways of discerning meanings in such behaviour.

Three useful concepts

I base my consideration of these matters on three concepts, namely, "non-verbal communication", "acting in", and "enactment". Representing different eras in the history of psychoanalysis and arising from different traditions within the field, these notions provide the conceptual framework for understanding and interpreting patients' actions in the clinical situation.

Non-verbal communication

The fact that patients communicate important information about their inner worlds by routes other than spoken words has been known since the beginning of psychoanalysis. In his treatment of Frau Emmy von N., Freud made the following eloquent observation:

> This lady, when I first saw her, was lying on a sofa with her head resting on a leather cushion. She still looked young and had finely-cut features, full of character. Her face bore a strained and painful expression, her eyelids were drawn together, and her eyes cast down; there was a heavy frown on her forehead and the naso-labial folds were deep. (Breuer & Freud, 1895d, pp. 48–49)

Freud's drawing significant inferences from this patient's facial expressions is, however, not the only evidence that he gave considerable importance to the patient's appearance and actions during the clinical hour. This is evident at many places in the Rat Man case where Freud (1909d) mentions his patient's facial expressions. Yet another evidence comes from his deduction (1917) that patients who leave the door to the waiting room ajar while entering the treatment office are expressing a conviction that no other patient shall come after them. All these illustrations pale, however, when juxtaposed with Freud's observations in "Remembering, Repeating, and Working-Through". He states that often:

> [T]he patient does not remember anything of what he has forgotten and repressed, but acts it out. He reproduces it not as a memory but as an action; he repeats it, without, of course, knowing that he is repeating it. For instance, the patient does not say that he remembers that he used to be defiant and critical towards his parents' authority; instead, he behaves in that way to the doctor. (1914g, p. 150)

Analytic pioneers following Freud continued to address the significance of communication via action. Reich (1933) paid keen attention to the physical dimension of character armour and underscored the stiffness of the paranoid, lyrical grace of the hysteric, and statuesque aloofness of the narcissist in the clinical encounter. Deutsch (1952) coined the phrase "analytic posturology" and devised stick figure "posturegrams" to capture the links between what the patients talked about and how they lay on the couch.

Nearly two decades later, Arlow (cited in Suslick, 1969) categorised non-verbal behaviours in the analytic situation into four types: (i) actions that serve as punctuations in the verbal material, (ii) actions that perform the function of a glossary and explain what the patient is saying, (iii) actions that serve as footnotes and enlarge the spoken words' reach, and (iv) actions that are automatic eruptions of dissociated mental activity. Of note here is that the first three categories assign a second-tier status to non-verbal communication; only the fourth allows it to stand as significant on its own merit. This inclination found greater attention in the works of Shapiro (1979), Anthi (1983), and McLaughlin (1987, 1992). The last-mentioned made non-verbal communication a focus of his attention and documented its great informative potential vis-à-vis the clinical process. McLaughlin's investigations extended beyond the ordinary emblems (conventional movements that are interpretable in the absence of speech) and gestures (bodily movements that are synchronised with speech) to include subtle and often unnoticed acts like cuticle picking, rubbing fingertips, touching the mouth, and crossing the legs during the clinical hour.[1]

Acting in

The term "acting in" comes from the early days of psychoanalysis. It was coined by Meyer Zeligs (1957) to distinguish "acting out" within the analytic hours from "acting out" outside the analysis. "Acting in" may be restricted to bodily movements and postural changes on the couch through which unconscious conflicts are manifested, or it may involve more elaborate behaviours which express repressed memories. Either way, it represents a "muscular expression of a thought process" (Zeligs, 1960, p. 411). It might manifest genetic or extra-transferential fantasies as well as unconscious transference-based desires (Paniagua, 1998). In either case, something is put into action instead of words. Viewed this way, "acting in" is a form of resistance. However, when the conflictual material pertains to the preverbal periods of childhood and has not had adequate psychic representation and "mentalisation"

(Fonagy & Target, 1997) to begin with, such behavioural communication might be the only manner through which it can find its way to the clinical surface. Here, "listening" to the communicative value of "acting in" takes technical precedence over underscoring its resistance potential. In this context, it is interesting to note that, in a later publication, Zeligs (1960) himself regarded "acting in" as a mid-point between "acting out" and free association.

Enactment

A popular term from contemporary psychoanalysis, "enactment" made an en passant appearance nearly forty years ago in a paper by Sandler, Dare, and Holder (1973). Lamenting the over-extension of the term "acting out", these authors stated that "It is perhaps unfortunate that some such term as 'enactment' was not used in the literature to distinguish the general tendency to impulsive and irrational action from acting out linked with the treatment" (p. 100). They could not have guessed that two decades later, "enactment" would gain immense popularity, especially in the North American psychoanalytic parlance.

Elsewhere (Akhtar, 2009), I have summarised the various different ways the term "enactment" is used. It is beyond the scope of this chapter to cover the vast literature on this topic and I refer the reader to Ivey's (2008) formidable review of the definitional ambiguities in the concept of "enactment" and also their technical implications. Here it would suffice to say that "enactment" has both "one-person psychology" and "two-person psychology" interpretations. The former perspective refers to the patient's putting his transference fantasies into actions rather than words (Hirsch, 1998) and is therefore a "new and improved" form of Zeligs's (1957) "acting in" concept. The latter perspective suggests that "enactment" happens when a patient has unconsciously induced the analyst to live out his transference fantasy. Boesky's (1989) characterisation of enactments as "behaviors which have an actualizing intention" synthesises these two perspectives in an economically prudent manner. All in all, it seems that a central feature of enactment is the transformation of wishes and fantasies into a behavioural performance which seems "real". Actions that fall under the rubric of enactment have not received "significant contributions by the ego's capacities for anticipation, frustration tolerance, or delay" (Jacobs, 1991, p. 32). It is for this very reason that such actions warrant analytic attention.

For didactic ease in explicating all that is communicated by the patient in the form of action, I will divide my discourse into listening to actions (i) while arranging the first visit, (ii) as the patient arrives for the first visit, (iii) during this initial consultation, (iv) during the beginning phase of analysis, (v) during the middle phase of analysis, and (vi) during the termination phase of analysis. I will conclude by summarising the observations made under these categories, entering some caveats, and indicating the areas that need further thought.

While arranging the first visit

Our first contact with a prospective patient is usually on the phone. Elsewhere (Akhtar, 2009, pp. 14–17), I have delineated the guidelines for responding to this first phone call. Here, what I wish to emphasise is that the conversation that ensues then can contain elements of action. By making this or that statement or by asking one or the other question, the patient might actually be *doing* something to the analyst: depositing something into him, causing him to regress, inducing shame, and so on. The spoken words then acquire the status of actions and these actions need to be listened to even more carefully than the words that embody them.

Clinical vignette 5

While setting up an appointment via telephone, John Schmidt asked me twice whether my office building had a name, such as the Pan Am Building, the Chrysler Building, and so on. I was intrigued by his insistence, since I had already given him the street number of my building. I also noted that both the buildings he mentioned were in New York and not in Philadelphia, where I practise. I politely repeated that my building did not have a name, keeping my sense of curiosity for later.

When he arrived, the first thing I learned was that his full name was John Schmidt, Jr. Next, I gathered that he had a pattern undermining his achievements, in the realm of both romance and business, just when success was around the corner. Much unconscious guilt seemed to lurk in his psyche. To look for the sources of such guilt, I turned to exploring his childhood. Now I learned that despite having an older brother, it was he who was named after his father. Upon my enquiring about it, he agreed that this was not customary but said that he had never thought about the reasons for this unusual situation. Further questioning revealed that his older brother was mildly developmentally delayed. At this point, I ventured a hypothesis. Could it be that his older brother had at first been named after their father, only to be given a different name after the discovery of his developmental delay? The patient was moved by this suggestion and, though he did not remember hearing any such thing while growing up, began talking about his sadness about his brother and his guilt over his own success, which he had impressively underlined on many occasions. As all this came pouring out, I became aware that he had unconsciously given me a clue to his problem by insisting on the phone that my building (me) have a bigger, better name than merely a number. I brought up our telephone conversation and pointed out that his insistence upon my building (i.e., I) having a better name was a disguised way of "returning" his borrowed name to his older brother. In essence, it was his way to repair the damage he had felt he had done. The patient began to sob and it was clear that he felt understood in a way that he had never experienced before.

Here, listening to the action that the patient was performing while setting up an appointment helped clarify and document the hypothesis that was later evolved during the interview itself.

Upon arrival at the office

Behavioural communication by the patient often becomes more "loud" as the patient actually arrives for the consultation. The clothes (e.g., too formal, too informal, too revealing) that the patient has chosen to wear on that particular day might tell a story by themselves. Delay in arriving or confusion about the time of appointment can also reveal important information about the patient's dynamics.

Clinical vignette 6

Having waited for Gina Spencer, who had sought a consultation with me, for about twenty minutes, I received a frantic phone call from her. She was looking for my office in a building five blocks away. Where did I say my office was? When I repeated my address, she realised her "mistake" and wanted to know if she could still come over for her appointment. Thinking that not much time would be left by the time she would have arrived, I offered her an appointment on a subsequent day. She apologised for her "mistake" and accepted my offer.

On the day before Gina's second appointment, I came out of my office after the last patient of the day had left to find her sitting in my waiting room. She was enraged and said that she felt very humiliated by my having "abused" her in this fashion! Puzzled, I asked what it was that she felt I had done to her. She responded by saying that I had kept her waiting for an entire hour while seeing another patient. It took her a few minutes to realise that she had come a day earlier than her scheduled appointment! Now, there were these two enactments even before we began a formal consultation. First, she went to the wrong building and was frantically looking for me. Second, she came at the wrong time and felt "abused" by me. I kept these in mind and decided to see what in our "third" encounter (i.e., our first formal interview) might shed light on the communications contained in these enactments. (Besides, of course, I noted the propensity to acting out, resistance, sadomasochism, and use of paranoid defences.)

In her subsequent appointment, for which she arrived punctually, Gina told me that her main difficulty was constant anger at men, sexual disinterest, and depressive mood swings with occasional suicidal thoughts. She revealed that her father, to whom she was very attached, had abruptly left the family when she was five years old. She never saw him afterwards and was always "searching" for him. When she was eight years old, her mother remarried. Her stepfather sexually abused her until she was thirteen years old. At this time, the patient moved out of the house and started living with an aunt. As this material came out, I brought to her attention that her frantically "searching" for me the first time and feeling "abused" by me the second time were perhaps her ways of putting me in the place of her real father and stepfather, respectively. Till the time I was in either position, I added, she could not relate to me. Perhaps she needed a third chance, a new experience. The patient began to cry and, after composing herself, revealed more details of her anguished life.

The point I am trying to make here is that enactments as gross as these cannot be ignored. They must be thought about and sooner or later brought up for discussion. Vigilance combined with tact is the key here. This applies not only to the patients' appearance and behaviour but also to the things that they bring along with them.

Clinical vignette 7

As Alex Bartlett, a thirty-four-year-old lawyer, entered my office for his first interview, I noticed that he was carrying a popular magazine in his hand. Sitting down, he put the magazine on the table near him. The session proceeded along conventional lines while, in a corner of my mind, I kept wondering about the magazine. Oblivious to my concern, he went on to describe the interpersonal difficulties that had led to his seeking help. He said while finding women was not difficult for him, keeping them involved certainly seemed a problem. One after another, they left him complaining of his aloofness and self-sufficiency. I found myself looking at the magazine he had brought along but decided to wait before saying anything about it.

Moving on to his family background, Alex revealed that his parents had divorced when he was four and, for the following three years, his mother toiled hard to raise him and his two older sisters. She worked long hours and expected the children to be well-behaved. Alex grew up to be a courteous young man who was repeatedly abandoned by women who found him nice but unengaging. He suffered greatly since he wanted involvement and mutuality in his life. At this point, I asked him about the magazine. He seemed surprised and said that he had brought it for reading in the waiting room. I asked him if he thought that I would have no reading material there and if he could see how this seemingly innocuous behaviour betrayed his anxiety about dependence and attachment. I added that perhaps it was this sort of "self-sufficiency" that was found unacceptable (and unconsciously rejecting) by his girlfriends. He was taken aback but could readily see the dynamics in action. His eyes filled up with tears and he said, "But I can't help it. I have always relied upon myself." Yet there was a clear sense in the office that an aspect of his problematic "character armour" (Reich, 1933) had already been made ego-dystonic.

Gina Spencer's confusion about the venue and time of the consultation and Alex Bartlett's showing up with a rolled-up popular magazine in his hand constituted "action clues" to important, if not central, aspects of their conflicts. The dialogue that unfolded during the interview proper allowed access to deeper material that could be linked to the behaviour preceding it. But what if the anamnesis had not given any hint as to what these behaviours meant? In that case, the observations would have to be "filed away" and kept as a background reference should some "explanation" to them appear later. All this, of course, raises the issue of technique with patients' actions and this is something I will keep touching upon in each section of this chapter and then present in a more succinct and pointed fashion towards its conclusion. For now, I suggest that we consider the actions that occur while we are conducting the first interview with the patient.

During the initial consultation

Communicating via behaviour does not stop with the patient's entering the office and taking the assigned seat. Indeed, some very important clues can be hidden in the manner that people sit down, the posture they take, and the behaviours they display—unbeknown to them—as opening gambits. The following two clinical vignettes illustrate what I have in mind here.

Clinical vignette 8

> Troy Blackwell, a twenty-four-year-old pharmacy student, sought consultation following some disciplinary problems he faced at his college. He arrived in time and was casually dressed in jeans and a tee shirt. As he was sitting down in the "patient's chair" in my office, he put his hand in his hip pocket and pulled out a packet of unfiltered Camel cigarettes and a somewhat dirty cigarette lighter and put them on the small glass top table that, at an angle, sat between him and me. "I didn't want them to be crushed," he explained. I nodded in agreement with this rationale (and rationalisation) while privately wondering about other potential meanings of this act. I also registered a mild feeling of annoyance at the "dirty stuff" (the exact words that came to my mind then) that he had put on my nice and clean table. Did the gesture portend that sadomasochism

was about to unfold between us? Was it a gauntlet and a challenge or was it an appeal to be contained? Or, both? And, how was all this related to the disciplinary problems Troy was facing at his college? It was only when he began talking about these and the fact that his teachers consider him "provocative" that I asked him if he regarded brandishing cigarettes in a doctor's office "provocative" or not? Troy smiled, winked, and said, "Touché!" (not registering that even his agreement was expressed in an overly casual manner).

That a small and unwitting (from the patient's point of view) act during the initial consultation can open up a line of deeper investigation is also documented by the following clinical occurrence.

Clinical vignette 9

Layla Aafandi, a thirty-year-old pharmacist of Iranian origin, came to her first interview in a revealing dress. The neckline of her blouse swooped down to reveal a major portion of her breasts and her skirt was up to her mid-thigh region. Even more strikingly, she "sat" on the chair in a nearly lying down posture. Her legs were extended and one of her feet came very close to mine. I was made uncomfortable by this and immediately suspected that she had been sexually abused as a child. However, I did not pull my foot back quickly. I waited, and went on to hear her story and collect pertinent information. Soon the history of childhood sexual abuse (by her father) came out. At this point, I gently withdrew my foot and pointed out that her manner of sitting, which created the possibility of physical contact between us, might have been related to what had happened in her past. Perhaps she was unwittingly inducing the discomfort of unwelcome proximity in me so that I could emotionally know what she had felt as a child. Besides, it seemed that she was also testing the safety of being with me. These remarks led to her sitting more erect, crying, and gradually revealing a history of much sexual exploitation, including two rapes, during adult life.

The following points need to be noted as far as the two foregoing clinical situations are concerned. In both instances, I (i) became almost immediately aware that the patient was trying to communicate something by an action, (ii) waited a while to see how this would unfold, (iii) did not respond by a counter-action, (iv) made an interpretive remark in the form of a gentle question, and (v) addressed the action only when supportive material for my hypothesis became available in the patient's spoken words. The beneficial impact of such a titrated response in creating and strengthening the "therapeutic" or "working alliance" (Greenson, 1965; Zetzel, 1956) is especially evident as the actual work of intensive psychotherapy or psychoanalysis gets started.[2]

During the beginning phase of treatment

The tendency to convey feelings by actions often intensifies when a patient gives up sitting and begins to lie down on the couch. The ensuing loss of visual contact increases the distance from the analyst. The analyst then has to be mindful of the effects of this upon the patient's feeling states and ego capacities, as well as of the defensive strategies mobilised by the patient to compensate for this increased distance between them. Talking rapidly and incessantly to strengthen contact with the analyst, curling up in a frightened ball to hold on to oneself, and mumbling inaudibly to evoke activity from the analyst are all actions that betray anxiety over this increased distance and should be understood as such, even if deemed not "ready" for interpretation. Unusual manifestations of anxieties pertaining to this sudden increase in distance should also be kept in mind.

Clinical vignette 10

> Jean Rosenbaum began to lie on the couch so that a significant portion of her face was visible to me, and I found myself repeatedly looking at her. I felt "pulled" to do so with an admixture of curiosity and mild anxiety. My understanding of this situation was multidetermined and included her childhood over-stimulation by parental nudity. Such reversal of anxious scopophilia into teasing exhibitionism seemed also linked to her distress at losing visual contact with me. However, since Jean was not talking about it (either directly or in derivative forms), I decided to wait and meanwhile bear the tension that her action was producing in me.

This raises another important issue of technique. The analyst's ability to discern a "deeper" meaning in an action of the patient (either derived from his familiarity with the patient's history or developed out of his clinical experience and psychoanalytic knowledge in general) does not automatically mean that he can go ahead and interpret along those lines. Early phases of treatment especially demand caution and it is better that the analyst restrict his or her interpretation to the "experience-near" and contextually immediate aspects of the patient's action. Even for that, one often has to wait for an opportunity; this may come in the form of the patient's own comments upon the action, associations that approximate the hypothesis that the analysis has meanwhile developed, or a parapraxis or dream with links to the action in question.

Clinical vignette 11

> Sylvia Smith, a thirty-six-year-old paediatric nurse, came to see me after a deepening involvement with a man began to make her anxious. Not that the relationship was bad or the man was not to her liking. It was just the opposite. She liked him immensely and was falling in love with him but was terrified of losing him and getting hurt. She said that she was taking him in "small doses" lest he abandon her. Suspecting hunger, insecurity, and guilt, I explored her early life history during the consultation and was not surprised to find that she had been sexually abused as a child by her uncle. And, when she told her mother, the latter refused to believe her.
>
> As our work progressed and she moved into analysis proper, I noted that she lay on the couch somewhat half-heartedly insofar as she kept one of her feet firmly planted on the floor. It was as if she was forever ready to get up and leave. This behaviour, perhaps, indicated anxiety about "surrendering" herself to the couch (with all the attendant fears of being abused), defence against her hunger for my attention (taking me in "small doses"?), and guilty refusal to reap all the benefits of being on the couch, able to free associate, and be listened to in a non-judgmental fashion.

In contrast to this unobtrusive one-foot-on-the-floor behaviour was the entirely unexpected offer of a gift by a patient within a few weeks of starting her analysis.

Clinical vignette 12

> At the end of a session in the second month of her analysis, Melanie Wright, an otherwise psychologically-minded young woman offered me a bag full of apples. She said that she had gone apple-picking over the weekend and wanted me to have some. I was taken aback. Neither her characteristic way of being nor the material in the session had prepared me for this. I responded, "I appreciate your bringing me this gift but I cannot accept it. See, our task here is to understand, enlighten ourselves to your mental functioning and, thus, come to grips with your difficulties. We cannot, therefore, move into actions, especially ones whose meanings are unknown to us. Now, I regret if my stance hurts your feelings, but I do not apologise because my intent is not to hurt you." She listened carefully and nodded in agreement. I then spontaneously added, "For instance, apples. What comes to mind about apples?" She answered, "Adam's apple! ... Adam and Eve ... forbidden fruit." She smiled, blushed, and left shaking her head, saying "I understand, I understand."

On the surface, this vignette shows how the steadfast maintenance of a therapeutic frame and "invitation" for the patient to become more curious lays down the foundations of a good alliance. It illustrates how even a partial interpretation of enactments during the beginning phase can enrich the patient's "observing ego" (Fenichel, 1941). At a deeper level, however, it also raises the interesting question of whether minor enactments during the beginning phase of analysis occur only after a reasonable working alliance has already developed between the partners of the clinical dyad. When, how, and how much to interpret remain the main clinical concerns, however. Take the following example as a potential instigator of such questions.

Clinical vignette 13

> Each time he rose to exit after his session was over, Randy McCall, a Texas-born internist in his fifties, stopped at the door, looked back at me and uttered the day and time of our next appointment. There was an ever-so-slightly questioning tone to this: "Tuesday, 2 p.m.?", "Wednesday, 4 p.m.?", "Friday, noon?", and so on. As he flung the

inquiry across the room, I, still seated in my chair, felt as if Randy had actually thrown a hook and was pulling at it so that I would have to nod in agreement. Moving my head up and down did not seem in my control; it was as if he was making me do it. Not nodding felt more like something I could do but then I would have to actively resist the pull from him. A few seemingly innocuous words from him had the impact of a powerful, though invisible, action.

Randy McCall was one of my "control" cases, that is, an analysand I worked with during my years of training to become an analyst. I was in weekly supervision with the renowned child analyst, Selma Kramer (1921–2000), at that time. Puzzled about the "correct" way of responding to my patient's behaviour at the end of each session and wanting to learn finer points of technique, I asked my supervisor for guidance. Should I nod? Or, should I make an effort to preclude my head from bobbing up and down? She laughed and told me to do whatever felt natural to me. Then she said—what seems self-evident to me some thirty years later—more important than nodding or not nodding were two other matters: (i) what is leading the patient to do this?, and (ii) what is my anxiety about yielding to his "demand"? Not quite able to go to the depth she was taking me, I insisted upon finding a behavioural recipe for my dilemma. "Should I bring it to his attention then?" I asked. She stood firm, saying that I ought to wait until material involving attachment, separation, loss, uncertainty about finding and re-finding love objects appears in verbal form. Only then should I comment upon his actions. In retrospect, I see the wisdom of her supervisory counsel.

An interesting footnote to this clinical experience is that nearly twenty years later, I encountered the exactly same behaviour in the early phases of analysis of a female analysand of Middle Eastern origin. Not only was I better prepared to deal with it then, I also noted that the propensity for acting (communicating) in this way cut across gender differences and cultural backgrounds. My faith in the universality of basic human anxieties and their communication via action deepened.

During the middle phase of treatment

Before getting into what sort of actions can occur during the middle phase of analysis and how one "listens" and responds to them, it might be worthwhile to spell out what we mean by the designation "middle phase". Since it is exquisitely unique for each patient—in fact, each clinical dyad—it might suffice to say that "middle phase" subsumes all that happens between the end of "beginning phase" and the onset of the "termination phase". Building on this proposal, I have elsewhere delineated the characteristics of the "middle phase" in the following manner.

> If this is correct, the onset of "middle phase" would be indicated by the crystallisation of fleeting transference reactions into transference neurosis. The "middle phase" would last until transference pressures on the analyst diminish, the patient's attention shifts towards the future, and reasonable evidence of major transferences having been worked through is demonstrated; in other words, when termination is in the air. Analytic work during the "middle phase" (e.g., Fenichel, 1941; Greenson, 1967) is characterised by consistent resistance analysis, deepening of transference-countertransference experience, dream analysis, *interpretive handling of enactments*, reconstructions, and, above all, the tedious process of working through by which the patient gains insight into how many different ways and with what self-deceptive ease he still remains vulnerable to his infantile longings; try new ways of acting, maintaining vigilance towards the potential for regression, and increasingly self-observant building up of core childhood conflictual issues with their adult life, and transferential re-creations are all tasks of the "middle phase". (Akhtar, 2009, p. 172, italics added)

Since the topic under consideration here is the patient's tendency to communicate by actions, it is the "interpretive handling of enactments" that matters most to us.

As transference deepens and regression sets in, dreaded scenarios created by infantile fantasies inch their way towards consciousness. In this process they produce anxiety since the ego, having relegated them to the cellar of dynamic unconscious, is now forced to manage the resulting drive upheaval. Measures deployed by the ego to handle this "new" material include further repression (failure of which results in telling parapraxes and dreams), negation (which lets the material appear in consciousness in its inverted form), and acting out (which lets some steam off and, under favourable circumstances, renders the remnant material accessible to interpretation). Empathic attunement with such second-tier defences facilitates the investigation of newer and developmentally earlier transference paradigms.

Clinical vignette 14

> Ruby Kaplan, a thin-skinned, fearful, and immensely needy, bor-derline young woman was in a five-times-a-week analysis. From time to time she felt a bit more confident of her acceptability to me. Usually this was a result of a piece of superego analysis, whereby the defensive nature of her inhibitions became more observable to her and she learned of the childhood roots and current uses of ter-rifying inner injunctions. Mostly, she was afraid of overburdening me and was immensely thankful for my attention. At other times, she expressed a need to see me more often, have longer sessions, meet me on demand, and so on. Five times a week for fifty minutes certainly did not seem enough. I encouraged her to tell me more about this. She revealed that as a child she felt horribly rejected by her mother, who sternly discouraged any physical contact between them. She sobbed. We went on in this staccato fashion.
>
> One day, Ruby revealed that she had found out where I lived and had driven by to take a look at my house. I experienced mixed feelings upon hearing this. Mostly, I felt fascination at this man-ner of the transference deepening. The link between this behaviour and her childhood wishes to touch her mother was clear to me. When I brought this to her attention, she noticed the connection, too. However, the material did not deepen. Enquiries what fanta-sies she had about my house, what or who she really wanted to see, what the house stood for, how the looking at my house might have been a way of avoiding wishes to see me more fully (she was on the couch) yielded meager results. Gradually, the pattern of visiting my house became a regular one. Three, four times a week, including weekends, she drove by the street on which I live, slowing down as she passed my house, looking at it intently. Once in a while, from inside my house, I could see her driving by in her car. I felt intruded upon and annoyed. Listening to the reports of these visits during her sessions, I was reminded of her wanting to see me more than five times a week, for longer sessions, and on demand. I wondered if behind such coercive control lurked the fear of having "killed"

me during the intervals? Or, was it a developmental need? In other words, was the patient's wish to have more contact a defence against repressed hostility or was her going to my house an innovative way of having more sessions, without which she felt utterly disorganised? Two interventions were thus possible. One leaned towards interpreting the defensive and/or provocative actions. The other involved acknowledging the adaptive aspects of her behaviour, which sought satisfaction of an ego need that I had failed to meet. I chose the latter intervention and it facilitated the progress of our work. The patient felt understood, came up with new memories, and gradually stopped driving by my house.

While this clinical vignette demonstrates the communicative significance of actions outside the confines of the clinical chamber, the following report by Pulver (1992) illustrates how changes in erstwhile posture and hand movements can betray a new development in the transference-countertransference axis during the clinical hour.

Clinical vignette 15

"A patient of mine had been describing at some length some egregiously nasty behavior of her mother, behavior that we were coming to see as illustrative of her mother's self-centeredness, critical nature, and inability to empathize with the patient's feelings and wishes. After her description of one incident that had particularly upset her, I asked her how she felt her mother had been feeling when she acted as she did. She tried to address this question, but there was a peculiar distance and deadness in her response. Her hands, previously gesticulating, were silent. Her entire upper torso, previously animatedly engaged in the description, now lay still on the couch, and there was a flattening in the tone of her voice. I commented on the change and asked whether it was connected with my question. She was interested in conveying to me the agony she felt when her mother was being outrageous, while I seemed to be more interested in her mother. Furthermore, there was a hint of criticism in the way I asked the question, as if I were saying, 'Stop feeling so sorry for yourself and pay a little attention to your mother.' And, I came to realize, I was to some degree doing just that. My overt intent had been to help the patient deal with her mother's behavior by understanding some of the feelings that were behind it. Without realizing it, however, I had become impatient with my patient's litany of complaints and was covertly telling her to shape up and be constructive. As she and I explored what had happened between us, she made the first step in a gradually dawning understanding of a pervasive process. The same thing that happened between the two of us often happened between her and her mother. Her mother's hostile behavior arose not just from her own hostility, but because my patient provoked her to irritation and criticism. This opened new vistas toward the understanding of my patient's intricate relationship with her mother." (p. 166)

Not all enactments are so explicitly transference-related.[3] In many cases the fantasies that the patient has repressed and now needs to bring forth for analytic consideration and ego mastery emerge almost out of the blue. One then sees an eruption of actions that, while traceable to the active transferences, appear largely as passages of the patient's "one-person psychology" narrative.

Clinical vignette 16

Millie Horowitz, an unhappily married businesswoman in her mid-forties, had sought help in an overwhelmed state following a financial disaster in the business she owned. On the surface, this was due to the ineptitude of her chief bookkeeper. However, it soon became apparent that the bookkeeper was stealing large sums of money from the business and this contributed to its downfall. Ms Horowitz expressed pained surprise at this betrayal and had never seen it coming.

As our work progressed, a pattern of her being deceived and exploited gradually emerged: the man she married turned out to be drug-addicted; her college-age son shocked her by declaring that he was gay; her extramarital lover was not single as he said, but married. The list went on. Besides masochistic gullibility (which resulted from an unconscious need for punishment), Ms Horowitz also displayed a vulnerability for frequent accidents, small and big.

The daughter of parents who were survivors of the Nazi Holocaust, Ms Horowitz had grown up feeling that any problem she faced as a child was of little consequence compared to what her parents had suffered. She felt guilty at having needs, wishes, and age-specific anxieties. She could not rely upon her parents. Counterphobic assertion of independence from the internalised version of this experiential trap led to promiscuity and drug abuse during adolescence. By mid-adulthood, she settled down somewhat but then got married to a drug addict and began dabbling again in drugs herself. At the time of her arrival at my door, however, she had been drug-free for a couple of years.

Major transference themes evolved around provoking me by abrupt cancellations, forgetting our appointments, and, at times, coming just barely before the allotted time was up. These communicative actions were interpreted as masochistic appeals for punishment and encouraged her to talk about what her "crimes" were for which she wanted to be punished. Around this time, Ms Horowitz began to lose things: car keys, cell phone, wallet. A couple of times, she arrived at my office identity-less, so to speak, and a bit dazed. These actions appeared to reflect her guilty identification with her Holocaust survivor parents. As I hinted at this possibility, fantasies of what had happened to them and what they had undergone came pouring out amid much emotional turmoil. As a result, our work reached a deeper level.

What these three vignettes demonstrate is that valiant containment as well as rigorous interpretive deconstruction constitute the optimal strategy of handling patients' actions during the "middle phase". However, this must not be construed to mean that *all* behaviours of the patient must *always* be subjected to interpretation. Nothing can be farther from my intent. To be sure, one observes and privately speculates about all the elements (including actions) of what is going on in any given session but when it comes to actually addressing something, one always has to pick and choose. Greed, even epistemological or "analytic greed", has no place in clinical work. The following vignette illustrates how leaving a behaviour unaddressed might, at times, be the best therapeutic option.

Clinical vignette 17

Debbie Stein, a twice divorced, highly successful attorney in her mid-sixties, developed a life-threatening illness during her analytic treatment with me. Repeated hospitalisations, many near brushes with death, and her compromised physical condition necessitated the conversion of psychoanalysis into psychotherapy; the frequency of sessions had to be reduced and she began sitting up in the chair. During one such session, I noticed that she had picked up a small trinket from the little table that sat between us and kept "playing" with it as she talked about her failing health and the alarming side effects of the anti-cancer medications she was taking. Considering the fact that Debbie was childless, had no man in her life, and was handling the hardship of serious illness and repeated trips to clinics and hospitals all alone, I sensed that her touching the trinket that belonged to me was a way of feeling alive and in contact with the world as well as of establishing soothing physical comfort with me. Perhaps she wanted a hug or at least that I hold her hand? If so, she had found a convenient and acceptable way to fulfil that wish. I saw little point in "spoiling" such gratification by interpretive intrusion.

Such exceptions notwithstanding, patients' actions during the middle phase generally do require analysts' intervention. Establishing links between action and fantasy, extratransference and transference realms, drive and defence variables, and memories and fantasies inherent in such actions, and then engaging the patient in a mutual examination of these links, pave the way towards working through such material. Done over and over again—now from this perspective, now from that—such intensive work prepares the ground for termination.

During the termination phase of treatment

With substantive diminution of transference pressures and ascendency of ego, ground is set for termination. Improved affect modulation, replacement of immature defences by more mature ones, cessation of repetitive dreams, and enhanced capacity for object relations characterise this phase. Yet another feature is the ego's greater ability for sublimation and impulse control. Major enactments are therefore uncommon in the termination phase, unless of course the patient has been particularly action-prone to begin with. Even otherwise, non-verbal communication retains its place and might require attention. Moreover, the frequent recrudescence of presenting symptoms during this phase can also provide a basis for significant "acting in".

Clinical vignette 18

Charles Tucker had entered analysis largely because of his conflicts with authority figures and the consequent instability of his employment situation. He expected moral and professional excellence from his superiors and, when they disappointed him, became very angry and caustic towards them. He prided himself upon being utterly reliable, honest to a fault, and exacting of his talents and industriousness. Charles's background revealed a life-long idealisation-disillusionment rage pattern in connection with his father who promised all sorts of "goodies", (e.g., "Of course, I will buy you a new bicycle", "I am going to give you my car the day you graduate high school", "You will see what a grand party I will throw when you get into medical school", and so on) but never delivered them. Charles's hopes were constantly aroused and dashed.

During his analysis, a central piece of work revolved around transference material derived from his anguished and yet hopeful relationship with his father. Charles expected me to be articulate, highly insightful, and to impress him with my mastery of psychoanalysis (his finding out that I had written a number of books in the field gave this transference pressure a certain kind of "plausible" patina). Instead, he found me plodding and devoid of wit and quotations from analytic literature. He felt let down and angry. Transference interpretations led to more memories from early childhood of his disillusionment with his father.

Alongside such transferences were those where *he* would promise me things and would fail to deliver (e.g., "Oh, I am forgetting the name of this author you'd love to read ... I will tell you tomorrow," but then he would "forget" to bring this topic up again (and its negative and positive Oedipal dimensions). Such role reversals also had to be interpreted. Gradual acquisition of ego-mastery over this realm and the wedge—drawn by insight—between the childish and the realistic perceptions of "bosses" resulted in improved relations at his workplace. Charles began to be more tolerant and empathic towards his seniors. In turn, they showed greater acceptance of him.

In the last month of his analysis, Charles paid his bill on time. Looking at the cheque—after he had left—I was shocked: instead of $2800, he had written $28,000. The next moment, I noticed that he had entered the amount correctly in words: "two thousand, eight hundred dollars." My emotional reaction was mixed: I felt a jolt of excitement at "receiving" $28,000—"Wow! So much money!"—but was quickly "disappointed" that, in reality, I would get only $2800. I felt like little Charles who had been repeatedly "hoodwinked" by his father. In the subsequent session, I brought this to Charles's attention and very soon, both of us were able to see how he had turned the tables around and enacted an identification with this bombastic father.

The relative ease with which enactments of the sort mentioned above can be interpreted is based upon the fact that their content has been worked through over and over again in the preceding phases of analysis. Such ease of interpretation is not the only characteristic of the termination phase handling of the patient's actions. The renewed hope of actualising transference fantasies can, at times, necessitate rigorous and piecemeal reconstruction all over again with the work coming to resemble that in the middle phase. Finally, the appearance of a gift from the patient's side—one that has been discussed earlier—in the last session of the analysis often contains an admixture of transference enactment alongside genuine gratitude in the "real relationship" with the analyst (Smolar, 2002). Here the former aspect has to be left unanalysed owing to tact and lack of time available. Needless to add, if the preceding work has gone well, the gift given by the patient would be largely appropriate and "realistic" in nature.

Concluding remarks

In this chapter, I have surveyed patients' communicative actions as these appear from the very beginning of the clinical contact through the beginning and middle phases of treatment to its termination. Throughout this discussion, I have provided illustrative clinical vignettes and attempted to demonstrate how such actions are "listened to" and technically handled. The closing and synthesising remarks that I would like to make now fall into six categories.

- First and foremost, it needs to be underscored that the separation of "action" from speech in the patient's communication has its limits. Actions can speak louder than words and spoken words can dodge their communicative functions and turn into actions (see Chapter Six for details on this). The sharp distinction between action and speech here has largely been for didactic purposes and should be taken as such.

- Second, since the patient is always "acting" (e.g., entering and leaving the office, sitting up or lying down, getting up to leave, paying the bill), the question as to which actions warrant analytic attention is a legitimate one to raise. In other words, what might be the markers of behaviours that are deemed suitable for such attention? The answer is threefold: (i) the behaviour is striking and unusual, if not outright bizarre (e.g., the patient refuses to sit down or comes in wearing no shirt), (ii) the behaviour is threatening to break the therapeutic frame (e.g., the patient refuses to reveal his name, frequently cancels sessions, tries to become violent), and (iii) the behaviour is the sole available data (e.g., when the patient is chronically and tenaciously silent).

- Third, the manner and extent to which the meanings of such behaviours can be discerned and communicated to the patient vary with the phase of the treatment. In the initial stages, interventions directed at patients' actions are gentle, attention-drawing, and narrative-enhancing. They are also restricted to the extra-transference realm. As the treatment proceeds, however, one can make deeper remarks and unmask the transference-based aspects of such actions. Reconstruction of the childhood roots of such actions and the meanings that lie behind them also becomes possible. While this is true, situations can arise "at the beginning of treatment in which an early and deep interpretation may be necessary to overcome a particularly tenacious resistance. Such moves, when utilized, are frequently the result, not of technical strategy, but of intuition" (Jacobs, 1991, p. 5).

- Fourth, the interpretive guidelines above must be accompanied by the recognition that not all actions—including those that are quite noticeable—need to be addressed and unmasked. Many simply need to be noted quietly, "tolerated", and left untouched (see clinical vignette 11).

- Fifth, it should be remembered that all analysts do not listen in the same way. Some focus upon the ebb and flow of the patient's associations. Some find their own associations to be a more reliable avenue to understanding the patient. Others are sensitive to silences and can unearth meaning in the most ordinary of pauses. Still others are experts on observing the patient's posture, hand and feet movements on the couch, and to kinetic clues in general. Therefore, the threshold of listening to actions set above turns out to be quite variable. Analyst-based variables also come into play here.

- This brings up the final point and that is that the discourse in this chapter has largely—though not exclusively—centred upon the patient's inner experience, especially as it is "translated" into and conveyed via motor discharge. Actions of the analyst have received less attention. Such actions, along with the analyst's feeling states and thought-reverie, form the topic of the chapter that follows.

Notes

1. In contrast to these contributors who focus upon the patient's non-verbal communications, Jacobs (1991) pays attention to the analyst's physical movements and postural changes during the session (see Chapters One and Four for details).

2. Implicit in such a stance is the regard for maintaining "optimal distance" (Mahler, Pine, & Bergman, 1975) from the depths of the patient's mind. I have elsewhere (Akhtar, 1992) discussed the technical significance of the optimal distance concept from the beginning to the end of the treatment (and, even afterwards) in detail.

3. Kleinian analysts would, of course, object to such a statement since they regard all associations (and therefore, all enactments) to be related to transference (Hinshelwood, 1989).

CHAPTER FOUR

Listening to oneself

The doctor's unconscious is able, from the derivatives of the unconscious which are communicated to him, to reconstruct that unconscious which has determined the patient's free associations.

—Sigmund Freud (1912e, p. 116)

So far in this book, I have focused upon how the analyst attends to the material offered by the patient (e.g., associations, actions, silences). Now I turn my attention to what, in tandem, goes on within the analyst's own mind and how an ongoing, careful scrutiny of it deepens the knowledge about the nuances of the clinical process as well as of the patient's concerns and desires. In customary psychoanalytic terminology, I am referring to the informative potential of the "countertransference" phenomenon. However, our theory has moved far ahead from its early days. The introduction of the concept of "projective identification" (Klein, 1946), the attention to the role of the analyst's empathy (Fliess, 1942; Greenson, 1960; Kohut, 1977, 1982; Olinick, 1969), and the emergence of intersubjective and relational perspectives (Mitchell, 1988, 1993; Mitchell Aron, 1999; Ogden, 1986, 1994; Stolorow & Atwood, 1978) have challenged the original ideas about countertransference (see below). It is therefore best to begin with a brief clarification of this heuristic shift and only then address the specifics of the analyst's experience that demand attention.

Countertransference, empathy, projective identification, intersubjectivity

Sigmund Freud (1910d) coined the term "counter-transference" to describe the feelings generated in the analyst "as a result of the patient's influence on his unconscious" (p. 144). He believed that such feelings arose from the analyst's neurotic difficulties, were a hindrance to the proper flow of treatment, and could be avoided if the psychoanalyst himself had been analysed. From this pioneering observation through subsequent elucidations by Freud himself and others to the contemporary views, the saga of "countertransference" has had many twists and turns. The following major shifts in the view of the phenomenon constitute the nodal points in this story.

- Freud (1912b, 1915a, 1931b, 1937c) repeatedly emphasised the limitations posed on the analytic work by the psychoanalyst's blind spots. Many subsequent analysts subscribed to this "narrow" view of countertransference and regarded it to be a hindrance. Fliess (1953), for instance, stated that "countertransference, always resistance, must always be analyzed" (p. 270). A. Reich (1951), Gitelson (1952), and Hoffer (1956) concurred. Even Winnicott (1960b), known for his emotional openness, described countertransference as arising from the analyst's "neurotic features which spoil the professional attitude and disturb the course of the analytic process as determined by the patient" (p. 17).
- Others (e.g., Sharpe, 1947) asserted that countertransference was not only ubiquitous but essential. Money-Kyrle (1956) referred to empathy as "normal" countertransference and Little (1960) declared that "without unconscious countertransference there would be neither empathy nor analysis itself" (p. 30). It is only through empathy that the analyst could establish transient trial identifications with the patient and emotionally grasp his stance. Empathy, the prerequisite for understanding the patient's experience and formulating interpretations about it, was later elevated by Kohut (1977, 1982) to be an intervention *per se* with narcissistic patients.

- Paula Heimann (1950) liberated the concept of countertransference from its negative connotations, placing it in the centre of psychoanalytic technique. She extended the concept to include *all* the feelings that the analyst experiences during the analytic session. According to her, "The analyst's emotional response to his patient within the analytic situation represents one of the most important tools of his work—[it] is an instrument of research into the patient's unconsciousness" (p. 81). While not ruling out that the analyst's blind spots, collusions, and undue indulgences or deprivations can be harmful to a patient, many other analysts (Fromm-Reichman, 1950; Little, 1951; Racker, 1953) confirmed that the data of countertransference can provide useful information regarding the patient and what is going on in the analytic process.
- Heinrich Racker (1953, 1957, 1958) broke the monolithic notion of countertransference by classifying the associated phenomena into direct and indirect types. "Direct countertransference" referred to the analyst's emotional response to the patient. "Indirect countertransference" referred to the analyst's emotional response to someone important to the patient (see also Bernstein & Glenn, 1978; Jacobs, 1983; Searles, 1979, in this regard). "Direct countertransference" had two subcategories called "concordant" and "complementary" countertransferences. The former included the analyst's empathic resonance with the patient's felt conflicts; this was, of course, more marked if the analyst had similar conflicts himself. The latter referred to the analyst's unconscious identification with some unfelt and projected part of the patient's psychic structure; the analyst's emotional experience in this case was "opposed" to that of the patient's. Joseph Sandler, Christopher Dare, and Alex Holder's (1973) reminder that the prefix "counter" is used in two different ways in the English language, namely to parallel (e.g., counterpart) or oppose (e.g., counterattack) something, is pertinent in this context. Other considerations in regard to the phenomenology of countertransference include its intensity (from mild to severe), duration (acute or chronic), and clinical visibility (gross or subtle).
- The "classical" position that countertransference was a manifestation of the analyst's unresolved conflicts soon gave way to the position that it was "the patient's creation" (Heimann, 1950, p. 83). This idea grew out of Klein's (1946) concept of "projective identification", an individual's depositing his or her unacceptable self-representations

(and their associated affects and aspirations) into the mind of a receptive Other. Such a view became quite popular, especially among the analysts working with severely regressed, borderline, and near-psychotic individuals. Kernberg (1984), for instance, declared that "the more regressed the patient, the more he forces the analyst to re-activate regressive features in himself in order to keep in touch with the patient ... The more regressed the patient, the more global will be the analyst's emotional reactions" (pp. 266–267). In contrast to Racker (1957), Kernberg suggested that countertransference under such circumstances emanates not only from the analyst's identification with the patient's projected object-representations but also from his identification with the patient's projected self-representations.

- There also occurred a shift in the degree to which "countertransference enactment" (Jacobs, 1986) was deemed inevitable. At first it was felt that the analyst should be able to monitor his affective responses to the patient, dip into them, and, from this, learn about the patient, himself, their interaction, and the analytic process. Gradually, how-ever, it began to be recognised that there is an "irreducible subjec-tivity" (Renik, 1993) to the analyst's experience; he shows a certain "role responsiveness" (Sandler, 1976) to the patient's externalisation and grasps the meaning of it analytically only on a *post hoc* basis. A converse problem also came to the fore. This involved the analyst's resistance to feeling strong affects in the clinical situation (Coen, 2002) and thus becoming unable to analyse the patient's material in its ver-ity and depth.

- The rise of relational and intersubjective perspectives (Benjamin, 1995, 2004; Mitchell, 1988, 1993; Ogden, 1986, 1994; Stolorow, Brandchaft & Atwood, 1987, 1992) put forward the novel idea that both transference and countertransference are essentially co-created. The fundamental proposition of these models is that the chief moti-vation behind mental activity is not to discharge instinctual tension but to seek relational connection and communication. Countertrans-ference, for their proponents, is not only ubiquitous and unavoid-able but an acceptable and useful feature of clinical work. More importantly, countertransference is equated with the dialectical interplay between the patient's and the analyst's subjective realities and the intersubjective reality that is created—on an ongoing and ever-shifting basis—by their interaction.

- More recently, Parsons (2007) has brought a fresh perspective to bear upon the concept of countertransference. He raises an important question: "If countertransference may originate from the analyst's psyche and hinder the analysis, or from that of the patient and be able to help it, might the analysis also evoke elements belonging to the analyst's psyche which can benefit the analysis? ... The new possibility that I am raising does not involve the demand on the analyst either to surmount an obstacle in himself, or to recognise a projective identification, in order to get the analysis back on track. The idea that unconscious aspects of the analyst's psyche stirred up by the analytic encounter may not impede the analysis but bring fresh creativity into it takes us beyond the usual conception of countertransference" (p. 1452). Fox's (1998) notion of "unobjectionable positive countertransference" is also pertinent in this context.

This brief synopsis of literature demonstrates that (i) emotional resonances with (and/or defence recoil from) the patient's material are to be expected, (ii) such experiences reflect the analyst's transferences to the patient, his empathy with the patient, his identification with the patient's projected parts, and the material that is co-constructed in the intersubjective matrix of their relationship, (iii) while an occasional and reflexive enactment might be unavoidable, recovery from it informs the analyst about the analytic process at a deeper level, and (iv) a steadfast vigilance regarding one's emotional participation in the process—without the loss of spontaneity—is necessary and can be a powerful ally of the analyst's work ego. Even Freud, who was initially wary of "counter-transference", came to implicitly advocate for this position when he stated that "everyone possesses in his own unconscious an instrument with which he can interpret the utterances of the unconscious of other people" (1913c, p. 130).

To help fine-tune this "unconscious instrument", the analyst needs to watch his inner experience under the following categories. Such categorisation is of course artificial and done here in the service of didactic clarity. Even so, I suggest that, in order to grasp the totality of his experience, the practising analyst has to listen carefully to his (i) associations, (ii) emotions, (iii) impulses, and (iv) actions. I will now take up each of these categories separately in some detail.

Listening to one's associations

As the patient begins to talk and the session gets underway, the analyst leans back and listens carefully to the patient's associations (see Chapter One), tries to make sense of his long and short silences (see Chapter Two), and keeps an eye on his subtle and gross motor activity (see Chapter Three). The analyst makes a conscious effort to organise and understand the patient's material in order to arrive at a "conjecture" (Brenner, 1976) about its potential meanings; this then becomes the stepping stone for his spoken interventions. Alongside such deliberate mentation on the analyst's part, there is a sort of "giving in" to the patient's productions, a kind of psychic malleability, and a "regression in the service of the other" (Olinick, 1969). This allows for a state of reverie in which free associations meander in and out of the analyst's mind. Oscillating between such "free-floating responsiveness" (Sandler & Sandler, 1998) and intentional scanning of his subjective experience, the analyst comes into deeper contact with the patient and with the preconscious and unconscious aspects of the clinical dialogue. By paying keen attention to his own associations, the analyst learns much that is of significance about the patient's pathology and about the moment-to-moment state of transference developments. The following clinical vignettes illustrate this point.

Clinical vignette 19

Marsha Nardozi, a highly schizoid woman in analysis, was once lying totally silent and still on the couch. As efforts on my part to encourage her to free-associate or even engage in a conversation, so to speak, had failed miserably in previous such occasions, I decided to take a more laid-back stance. I let her be the way she felt "comfortable" and waited. The office was utterly quiet. Marsha lay still on the couch, motionless; it was hard even to tell if she were breathing. Then a childhood memory floated through my mind. This pertained to an elementary school trip to the local museum when I was eight years old. I was especially excited about seeing the Egyptian mummy that I had heard was kept there. However, when we reached the museum, I met an immense disappointment. Arriving at the room where the mummy was kept, all we could see was a glass box in which there was a tightly closed wooden casket in which there, supposedly, was a cloth-wrapped mummy. It was all too distant. Not seeing the mummy, in its morbid majesty, I was crushed. Waking up, as it were, from this dream-like state of mine, I returned to the self-reflective stance of an analyst. I became aware that there was a "mummy" present right this minute in the office; Marsha, in effect, was dead. Perhaps she had been killed by someone. Or, perhaps, she was telling me "Look, I am already dead, don't kill me." And, of course, the life of my analytic self was also threatened with extinction. To be true, such "insights" were helpful in enhancing my validity of the patient or at least in coming up with a plausible conjecture about it. But could these be conveyed to the patient?

Clinical vignette 20

Bill Trenton, a borderline young man in twice weekly psychotherapy exploded with rage when I refused to yield to his request for painkillers. In a menacing tone, he threatened to take my eyeballs off and crush them under his shoes. As I listened, there floated into my mind a picture of myself as a Raggedy-Ann doll (note, the female doll, perhaps standing for mother transference) lifted up by him as he enucleated my eyes. That the enactment was recapitulating a cruel parent-child interaction from Bill's early years was evident by the size differential between us (in the fantasy) and the associated dehumanisation (by the doll imagery) in the countertransference. Moreover, Bill himself seemed to be undergoing a diabolical transformation into a torture machine. The Raggedy-Ann doll image informed me about the nature of the self-object representations active in the transference-countertransference axis. But how—and, to what extent—to use such understanding in the intervention I would make remained an open question.

Clinical vignette 21

As Caroline Smith, a tall and attractive woman in her early thirties, began analysis, I became aware very soon that she came wearing the same clothes every day. Not only the attire was literally the same day after day, it was inelegant and made her appear less attractive than she could have been. Looking at her head on the couch's pillow from the seat behind her, I was also keenly aware that her hair was not shampooed. And, I found myself wishing that she would wash her hair, change her clothes, and improve her appearance. In fact, from time to time I imagined her in a long flowing gown, her long hair gleaming as it fell on her shoulders, her face with make-up, and her fingernails and toenails beautifully painted. My reverie would be broken each day by her appearance in the same dirty clothes as before. And, of course, I wondered about the origins of this 'vision' (Akhtar, 2009; Loewald, 1960). How much of it emanated from my own wishes (and, my impatience with her unkempt appearance) and how much of it was a reflection of Caroline's unverbalised longings to shed her masochism?

The important question these clinical vignettes raise is this: what can (and/or should) the psychoanalyst do with his own free associations during the clinical hour?[1] Can he reveal them to his patient? Or must he save them for his own use, for comparing and contrasting them with what occurs to him later on in the session (or, in subsequent sessions)? I suspect that different analysts handle such issues differently. I, for one, have found myself disclosing a snippet of my associations right *after* the patient has arrived at a certain understanding which, to both of us, seems correct. For example, I might say, "You know, just when you connected this feeling of guilt to your mother, I was thinking about the incidence when you were ..." In contrast to such "confirmatory" disclosure of one's association is what Bollas (1992) recommends: a judicious sharing of one's free associations to nudge the analytic process for it to move ahead. He notes that such practice is perhaps more common than ordinarily acknowledged, though such spontaneous and unformulated revelation of the analyst's associations is often mistaken for an interpretation. Bollas emphatically distinguishes the two.

> When the psychoanalyst tells the analysand of a spontaneous thought or memory that he is having in response to the patient's material or presence, this is his *selective* disclosure of a free association. If he has assembled many associations and observations into a conscious understanding of the patient's material, this is an interpretation proper. (Ibid., p. 113, italics in the original)

Bollas strongly recommends that the disclosure of the analyst's free association not be made (i) while the patient's dynamic process is smoothly unfolding and the patient is talking without any observable hesitation, (ii) in the spirit of largesse and "friendship", and (iii) with the implicit requirement that the patient respond to it. Instead, the disclosure should be (i) selective, (ii) related to the patient's material, (iii) unformulated, the raw data of the analyst's mind, (iv) constitute "a preconscious link to the unconscious latent thoughts" (ibid., p. 116) of the patient, and (v) followed up by a careful assessment of the patient's use of it (see also the views of Jacobs, 1991, described in Chapter One).

Listening to one's emotions

Another aspect of the analyst's subjective experience during the clinical hour is that of his emotions. Mobilised by events transpiring in the multifaceted matrix of the clinical dyad, the analyst's affects belong to three categories: (i) emotions felt *towards* the patient, (e.g., love, hate, affection, tenderness, concern), (ii) emotions felt *with* the patient (e.g., sadness, or happiness based upon empathic resonance), and (iii) emotions felt *on behalf of* the patient (e.g., feelings consequent upon projective identification of what the patient cannot bear within himself). Being aware that such developments can occur and being curious about their origins when they do, can yield meaningful information about the patient's dynamics and structural organisation.

Clinical vignette 22

Brooke Aggers, an 18-year-old college freshman, who sounded like a child while making an appointment on the phone, gave me a jolt when she arrived for the consultation. Opening the door to welcome her in the office, I immediately noticed how skimpily she was dressed and how much flesh she was showing. The "shock" I felt was—embarrassing to admit though it is –due to intense voyeuristic desire and sexual greed; guilty self-loathing soon followed.

By the time she sat down and began talking about what had brought her to see me, I had gained composure and began to wonder about the potentially co-constructed nature of my feelings. Now I looked at her face and found it to be a very sad child's face. The discrepancy in the desperate body display and the tear-filled eyes was striking. The saga that unfolded consisted of a dread of being found uninteresting by a much older boyfriend, feeling like a misfit in the big city (having recently arrived from a semi-rural area), and, most importantly, experiencing chronic discomfort with a heavy-drinking father whom she had frequently caught looking at her in a lecherous manner. Now, I began to feel sad as well as quite concerned for her.

In this instance, my intense desire to look at her exposed body and my sexual greed emanated from a "role responsiveness" (Sandler, 1976) which led me to react towards her like her father had done on numerous occasions. That my "induction" in this role took place *before* I had learned anything about her background speaks volumes as to how, via unconscious manoeuvres, people convey messages about their inner state to others. The two subsequent emotions—guilt and a feeling of composure that characterises my usual analytic stance—can be seen as the result of "disidentification" with her lecherous father introject and re-establishment of self-object boundaries on my part. Notable is the fact that these movements were purely affective and not accompanied by words in my mind. The same is true of the sad and protective feelings that emerged in me as the interview proceeded. Such wordless subjective cues are important allies of the analyst insofar as they can provide significant information about the patient's internal world. At times, these affective moments are subtle and nuanced, at other times loud and powerful. At times, such emotions are triggered by something the patient says or does (as in the vignette above) and, at times, these are the consequence of the analyst's own interventions.

Clinical vignette 23

Andrea Roberts, a narcissistic lawyer, spent the first two years of her analysis with me in a "cocoon transference" (Modell, 1975). She came regularly but seemed completely unrelated to me. Nothing I did or said seemed to affect her. I plodded along, waited. In the third year of her analysis, I had to take a few days off on short notice. She took the news in her characteristically nonchalant fashion. However, she began the next session by saying that a client had cancelled an appointment that morning and she had some free time in hand. She started going through her desk and came across a home insurance policy she had bought a few months ago. She was disappointed to discover that it was full of loopholes.

Now, hearing what appeared to be a thinly-disguised allusion to my going away, I felt a surge of excitement. My usual sense of boredom with her evaporated; I felt alert, involved, and mentally agile. I said, "Perhaps it is easier for you to talk about an insurance policy with loopholes than an analysis with sudden interruptions." A strange thing happened, though, as I was uttering those words. Midway in what had seemed to me an astute interpretation, I began to have a feeling that I was off the mark, and, by the time I finished speaking these twenty words, I "knew" that I had somehow hurt the patient. Andrea remained quiet for a while in response to my intervention. Then responded in a pained voice, "I can see how you arrived at what you said but it hurt my feelings because I was really worried about the policy and it seems that you were not paying attention to my concern about it."

It was evident that in quickly unmasking what lay behind a derivative of her feelings about our separation, I had overlooked the patient's need for such disguise. I had disregarded her need to control the boundaries between her conscious and unconscious psychic life and to yield such control at her own pace. In part this happened because I succumbed to the feeling of "analytic happiness" that came over me on recognising that this narcissistic woman was after all displaying evidence of being attached to me. My interpretation was in effect a countertransference enactment. The second affective movement in my subjectivity happened when—halfway through making the interpretation—I realised that I was hurting her. This was a preconscious recognition of my having been analytically greedy as well as an empathic attunement to the as-yet unspoken resentment of the patient. Post hoc as these insights were, such "listening" to my emotions deepened the understanding of my patient's exquisite need to regulate the emergence of attachment-related affects into her consciousness.

Listening to one's impulses

Besides the associations and affects one goes through while listening to the patient, a highly informative and technically useful subjective experience is constituted by feeling impelled to do something. The analyst might feel a pressure to act in a loving or hostile manner, for instance; impulses to affectionately caress or hug the patient are frequent ones among the former type. Impulses to deride, mock, and even hit the patient are frequent ones among the latter type. The intensity and duration of such impulses vary. They can be weak and fleeting or strong and tenacious. Faced with the latter, the analyst might feel distracted, exert mental effort to suppress the risk of acting upon them, and, in the process, lose contact with the patient. The fact, however, is that—unless the analyst is characterologically impaired—experiencing such impulses is due to his having come into contact with some deep aspects of the patient. Something disowned and repudiated within the patient has come alive, as it were, within the analyst's subjectivity.

Clinical vignette 24

Melanie Wright, a boyish young woman (also mentioned in Chapter Three) had sought treatment owing to feelings of anxiety and some marital tension. She had panicked when her husband was laid off from his job and, even though he was able to find gainful employment soon afterwards, remained anxious; in fact, she feared that they would become destitute. She and her husband frequently argued over this fear of hers and the friction between them was growing.

What struck me most when I first met her, however, was not this undue anxiety but the fact that she—a young woman in her mid-twenties—looked like a teenage boy. Making a mental note of it, I proceeded with gathering some background history. It turned out that her parents were divorced when she was six years old and that she had been raised by a loving but industrious and busy professional mother. Two other important facts were that the divorce had been precipitated by her father's announcement that he was gay and that young Melanie had to grow up with a very difficult older brother who constantly and, at times, physically hurt her. All sorts of factors, it seemed, worked in unison and led to the compromise of her femininity. The fact that she had been married for three years and seemed to love her husband appeared a little out of place.

As we began an analysis, I found myself experiencing something I had never felt during a clinical hour before. With Melanie talking—sometimes haltingly and at other times freely—about this or that issue, I experienced a peculiar discomfort in my rib-cage and upper abdominal area. It was as if someone was tickling me very hard (my mind went to some childhood memories that involved my older brother). I repeatedly wanted to change my position in the chair, as if to evade this tickling. Alongside such physical unease, I also felt impulses to interrupt her by saying something absurd and totally unrelated to what Melanie was talking about. If, for instance, she was talking about her parents' divorce, I felt like asking her if she knew the capital of Iowa and if she ruminated on her financial future, or I had the urge to tell her about the intricacies of Urdu poetry.

While I kept such impulses in check, the experience was nonetheless unnerving. I kept wondering what it was about. What would be the impact upon her where I to utter my passing thoughts? To be sure, she would be shocked. She might experience me as bizarre, if not outright mad.

A few weeks of sitting upon such impulses, waiting, allowing the material to evolve further, and conducting piecemeal defence analysis led to her revealing that her father had not only become gay but quite "crazy": he had painted the living and dining room ceilings purple, had started inviting his gay lovers to their home and would have sex in front of Melanie and her brother (when the mother was out working). Once or twice, he invited the children to join him and his lover in the bed while they were making love. As this material emerged—amid much distress and crying—I found a sudden reduction in my impulses to "act crazy"!

With the countertransference tension more in control, I became better able to think about what had transpired between the patient and myself. My "conjecture" (Brenner, 1976) was that the patient had been shocked by her father's perverse behaviour and had internalised this traumatic object-relations scenario. It remained "unmetabolised", however, and needed to be deposited into me, like Bion's (1962b) beta elements, for my containing and processing. She could retrieve it only after her capacity to bear the trauma and to "mentalise" (Fonagy & Target, 1997) grew. Meanwhile, I had to bear the noxious experience alternately as the victim (e.g., my feeling mercilessly tickled) and the perpetrator (e.g., my wishing to shock her by uttering absurdities) of the psychic violence.

Projective identifications (Joseph, 1987; Kernberg, 1967; Klein, 1946) of such a sort are, however, not limited to aggressively-tainted scenarios.

Subtle, iridescent, and yet unacceptable activation of (long-forgotten or wished for) internal good objects can also give rise to ego-dystonic impulses in the analyst, even though these are "loving" in nature.

Clinical vignette 25

> Olga Bokor, a Polish émigré scientist, sat on the couch (yes, she was not lying down that day) and broke into soul-wrenching sobs and tears. She was undergoing a very bloody divorce and with not a single relative in town—or even the country—was feeling awfully alone. Olga's husband, a narcissistic and paranoid man, had her trapped in a legal-financial corner. This was a nightmare to which her own masochism had contributed, no doubt.
>
> More to the point for matters under discussion here is the fact that watching her break down so badly, I felt a strong urge to get up from my chair and hold her in my arms. It seemed right. Surely, in the haven of my tight embrace, she would calm down, settle herself, and become more peaceful. The impulse was strong and certainly appeared humane. Resisting it in my mind, however, also revealed that I also looked forward to the sensual pleasure of having her trembling body against mine. There was some self-interest here too, it seemed. And, in just a little distance, sex. I decided to sit upon my impulse. Gradually, it passed. She, too, became more composed.
>
> Next day, a far more relaxed, if not beaming, Olga appeared in my office. She announced that upon leaving my office the previous day, she somehow felt better, stronger, and empowered. As if someone was truly on her side. As if she were not alone. Buoyed by such feelings, she fired her inept divorce lawyer and called a highly recommended attorney of great repute in the area. "Had you not been with me the way you were yesterday, I don't think I could have done this," she said.

As in the previous example, here, too, tolerating the impulses mobilised in the countertransference and not acting upon them proved to be useful. Moreover, it seems that the wish (to hold her) on my part did get conveyed, somehow or the other, to her; perhaps the resolute abstinence itself came across as firm "holding" (Winnicott, 1960b) and accomplished the auxiliary ego function desperately needed by the patient. Did I ask the patient if this were the case? No. That would have been analytically greedy and, by making the "holding" function a topic for intellectual discussion, would, paradoxically, rob the experience of its value. This was the kind of stuff that, in each session, we leave uninterpreted, while focusing upon other material. Such discretion, "tact" (Loewenstein, 1951; Poland, 1975), and choice upon what to focus and what to leave alone are integral to our daily work. More often than not, we are able to contain our impulses and learn about the patient (and ourselves) from this.

Listening to one's actions

While our impulses to act out during the clinical hour do teach us about what is going on in the transference-countertransference axis, at times, learning of such type occurs only after we have put something into action. Such actions are remarkably diverse; these can be minute and almost unnoticeable or gross and striking. Some remain limited to a raised eyebrow, leaning forward in the chair to speak, and raising one's voice. Jacobs notes that:

> Changes in posture, as well as other bodily movements, may be motivated by a number of factors, including muscular fatigue and physical discomfort, long-established movement patterns that are characteristic for any individual, as well as stimuli that arise as the result of personal preoccupations and conflicts. Nevertheless, if it is true that the analyst, seeking to understand the patient's unconscious communications, is able to utilize the thoughts and fantasies that arise in his own mind to assist him in this process, it would seem justifiable to assume that another pathway for the expression of his unconscious mental activity, namely that of motor discharge, can claim similar validity ... When the unconscious of the analyst is in tune with that of the patient—when in short he's listening well—certain aspects of his bodily movements, reflections of his own resonating mental processes, will occur in response to the patient's associations .... The analytic situation in which the analyst's full faculties are geared towards empathic understanding and in which temporary ego-regressions take place as an inherent part of the listening process, fosters the re-awakening of what we might term *body empathy*. (1991, pp. 105, 111, italics in the original)

Such empathy needs to be accompanied by vigilance towards one's somatic reactions. These might be well-attuned responses to the patient's material or "mini-countertransference" (Wolf, 1979) enactments. Only an honest self-searching can tell which is truly the case. Even greater attention needs to be paid to clinical actions that happen "accidentally". Such parapraxes can reveal a lot about the deeper undercurrents of transference-countertransference phenomena.

Clinical vignette 26

Caroline Smith (also mentioned in clinical vignette 2) was encouraged to seek treatment by her boyfriend. The issue at hand was her intense jealousy which he felt—and she, half-heartedly, agreed—was beginning to destroy their relationship. Caroline told met that they were "fine" and had a great time when together by themselves. It was in the company of others that she felt tense. She worried that he was looking at some other woman and taking too much interest in her. "Does he like that woman more?" "Is he thinking of having sex with her?" "Would he leave me?" Doubts and questions filled her mind. She was in agony.

Caroline's family consisted of a submissive, martyr-like, masochistic mother, a philandering and boastful father. An important formative event in Caroline's life was the family's discovery (when she was eleven years old) that her father was having an affair. Caroline's mother was at first devastated but rather quickly "forgave" her husband. Caroline, in contrast, never regained her love and respect for him. Matters were made worse by two other subsequent affairs and the revelation of yet another in the father's past, when Caroline was six years old. Feeling increasingly embittered at the father's philandering and, even more so, at her mother's tolerance of it, Caroline "decided" to never let this happen to her. She became vigilant—in fact, mistrusting and suspicious—about the behaviour of any man she dated. There was always another woman waiting to snatch him, as it were.

It was in the setting of such development background and constant complaining about her current boyfriend's looking at other women that I made a big error. One day, due to reasons beyond my control, I had to cancel our appointment. I called her and left a message to the effect, with appropriate sense of regret. However, as soon as I hung up, I realised that I had addressed her by another female patient's name!

The technical dilemmas that such a countertransference enactment posed were myriad. Should I call her back immediately and apologise? Should I wait till she comes for her next appointment? In the latter circumstance, should I open the session by acknowledging my mistake, apologising, and then asking for her reactions and associations? Or should I wait for her to bring the matter up, then apologise, and after that explore all that transpired between us? Note here that the issue of apology figures in every conceivable scenario that comes to my mind. This warrants a comment.

In discussing the place of apology in psychoanalysis, Goldberg (1987) delineated two possible stances. *One stance* holds the analyst to be more informed about "reality" and thus viewing transference, however plausible its content might be, as a distortion of that reality. In this perspective, the differences in perception between the patient and the analyst never call for an apology from the analyst. *The second stance* emanates from the analytic perspective which suggests that via empathic immersion, the analyst may attain an ability to see the patient's world as he or she does and the major burden of achieving and sustaining such intersubjective agreement rests upon the analyst. In this view the failure of intersubjectivity would largely be the analyst's responsibility and thus necessitate an apology from the analyst. Deftly and convincingly, Goldberg argued the untenability of either extreme position, concluding that while the wish to apologise may be countertransference based, it does have a place at certain times in certain treatments. Of course, the patient's experience of the analyst's apology needs to be then explored and handled in a relatively traditional way.

The important issue, therefore, was to understand my parapraxis, both in its motivational basis and its interpersonal gravity. It is only by careful self-scrutiny and self-analysis that the nature and meaning of such enactment could become clear. As I began to think along those lines, it occurred to me that I had "actualised"[2] my patient's central fear. I had betrayed her by bringing another woman between us and had become the philandering father and the boyfriend with the roving eye. And what I had done was (or, at least, could be) quite hurtful. I decided that I would apologise and then explore the material further. However, when the patient came for her next hour, she appeared to be largely un-offended. Not finding any direct or disguised mention of my error in her material, I asked if she had noted that I had, by mistake, called her by a name other than hers. She brushed it aside as just an ordinary mistake of a "busy" doctor. Was this dismissal genuine? Or was she behaving like her forever forgiving, masochistic mother? Clearly all this needed to be worked through in a piecemeal fashion in the subsequent period of our work.

In sharp contrast to the consciously unintended actions of such a sort are the "interpretive actions" (Jacobs, 2011; Ogden, 1994) which are performed deliberately and with a verbally formulated hypothesis existing in the analyst's mind. Their intent is to convey an interpretation to the patient. In Ogden's words, it constitutes

> the analyst's communication of his understanding of an aspect of the transference-countertransference to the analysand by means of activity other than that of verbal symbolization. At times such activity is disconnected from words (e.g., the facial expression of the analyst as a patient lingers at the consulting room door); at times the analyst's activity (as medium for interpretation) takes the form of "verbal action", for example, the setting of the fee, the announcement of the ending of the hour, or the insistence that the analysand put a stop to a given form of acting in or acting out; at times, interpretive action involves the voice, but not words (e.g., the analyst's laughter … interpretive action is not an exceptional analytic event; it is simply part of the fabric of ordinary interpretive analytic work … An important aspect of interpretation is the analyst's consistent formulation for himself of the evolving interpretation in verbal terms. (1994, pp. 108, 110, 123)

While the idea of "listening to oneself" does not seem to apply to such "interpretive actions" since one has (presumably) already thought them out, the fact is that one's original formulation is often incomplete. The response of the patient informs us about the nature of our "interpretive actions" and later self-reflection further clarifies their meaning. Take a look at the following vignette.

Clinical vignette 27

Jasmine Brooks, a doctoral student in her late twenties, was in analysis with me for over six years when the incident I am about to report took place. Before going into it, however, it might be worthwhile to give some background details on our work. Jasmine had sought help because of a paralysing inability to date and form romantic relationships. She felt intense anxiety about her appearance. While "average" in looks (and, at times, quiet good-looking), Jasmine regarded herself as ugly and utterly undesirable as a romantic and sexual partner. Analytic work proceeded haltingly with a powerful, idealising father transference giving way to the emergence of an intensely hostile sadomasochistic mother-daughter relationship from the earliest years onward. Jasmine expressed a desire to be married to me (as the appealing Oedipal father) but feared—indeed, was often convinced—that I despised her and found her to be repulsive (like she felt her mother had). Nearly six years of turbulent analytic work (consisting of "holding", affirmative interventions, transference and genetic interpretations, reconstructions, etc.) had only partly succeeded in resolving her difficulty. A certain "soft spot" remained. She was vulnerable to regress to feeling ugly and, frankly, to exploit this for sadomasochistic aims in the transference. Her complaining about her appearance was often so intense that it was I who felt violently beaten by it. To be sure, there were times when she would renounce this position, see herself realistically, and begin to make advances in her actual psychosexual life. However, guilt would soon take over since sexuality, for her, was hardly free of the connotations of Oedipal triumph. She would regress, as a result. The cycle would go on.

One day, while she started complaining about being ugly and I began feeling violently beaten by her attacks (seemingly against herself), I tried to inject some reality testing in the discourse. This was especially since we had analysed this matter for the umpteenth number of times and even agreed upon its fantasied nature. I said, "Let us see, are you talking about 'little Jasmine and her mother'? Or are you talking about 'Ms Jasmine Brooks and Dr Salman Akhtar'?" She responded in a defiant tone, "The latter. It is all real, you know." Upon this, I extended my hand from behind the couch and said, "On this insight, I congratulate you and would like to shake your hand." With a hefty dose of irony, I had sought to draw a wedge between her regressed, nearly psychotic ego and her intelligent and generally realistic self. Jasmine, however, responded by yelling at me. She said, "How can you offer to touch me? You are a psychoanalyst. You are not supposed to do that." I responded by saying, "A minute ago, I was a good psychoanalyst and a bad man. And you were focusing upon the latter while overlooking the former. Now, I am a good man and a bad psychoanalyst, and you are focusing upon the latter. How come you always find something bad in me and overlook the good?" Jasmine angrily responded that she was not interested in such talk. I asked her, "How come?" And the session went on.

My intent (at least, consciously) in offering to shake her hand was to demonstrate that not only was her insistence that I would never even imagine touching her incorrect but that it was being used quasi-deliberately in the service of a sadomasochistic transference. I regarded what I did to be an "interpretive action" (Ogden, 1994). However, upon later reflection (over the subsequent weeks and months), I began to see that the aggression contained in my counter-assertion was hardly all "neutralised"; there was a certain amount of hostility on my part as well which contaminated the implicit irony in the situation with a hint of mockery. Awareness of this dimension led me to question the thin boundary between "interpretative action" and "countertrans-ference enactment". Where does one end and the other begin? Most likely the distinction between them is not categorical but qualitative, in that the two exist simultaneously, though to varying degrees in a given instance. Ergo: the interpretive accomplishment of countertransference enactment should not be overlooked nor should the enactive aspects of interpretive actions. Follow-up work with the patient and with oneself is essential and informative in both instances.

Concluding remarks

In this chapter, I shifted my attention from listening to the patient's material (see Chapters One, Two, and Three) to the sort of informa-tion the psychoanalyst can draw from "listening" to his own self. I reviewed the broad and evolving concept of countertransference, under the rubric of which the experiences I described tend to belong. For didactic ease (though admittedly with undue precision), I catego-rised the psychoanalyst's informative self-vigilance into (i) listening to one's associations, (ii) listening to one's emotions, (iii) listening to one's impulses, and (iv) listening to one's actions. Through all this and more, I have attempted to clarify how the analyst's paying attention to his subjective experience is a rich source of information about the nature of his analysand's communications as well as the silently unfolding events in the transference-countertransference axis. Awareness of how one's subjective experience can be "inspected" from various perspectives is helpful to the analyst through emotionally turbulent times but what matters more is the experience he has had in his personal analysis (and the moral and conceptual integrity of his ongoing self-analysis). Heimann's reminder is pertinent in this context.

> The aim of the analyst's own analysis is not to turn him into a mechanical brain which can produce interpretations on the basis of a purely intellectual procedure, but to enable him to *sustain* the feelings which are stirred in him, as opposed to discharging them (as does the patient), in order to *subordinate* them to the analytic task in which he functions as the patient's mirror reflection. If an analyst tries to work without consulting his feelings, his interpretations are poor. (1950, p. 81, italics in the original)

By utilising a synthesis of the ego-psychological, object-relations, and the *au courant* relational and intersubjective vantage points, I have tried to extend the foregoing idea in useful directions. The same conceptual scaffold would help deepen our understanding of how—and under what circumstances—our capacity for analytic listening gets seriously compromised. This constitutes the topic of the next chapter.

Notes

1. Sharing his associations (or, snippets of them) poses even more complications for the analyst whose mother tongue is different from that of the patient. I have elsewhere (Akhtar, 2006) discussed this situation in some detail.

2. The term "actualisation" is used in psychoanalysis in three different ways: (i) when a growing child's fantasies are given credence by an event in the external reality, (ii) when an individual transforms his wishes and daydreams into a concrete, creative product, and (iii) when an analyst momentarily lives out the transference attributes assigned to him by the patient. My use of the expression here is in this third context.

CHAPTER FIVE

Listening poorly

"We have noticed that no psychoanalyst goes further than his own complexes and internal resistances permit"

—Sigmund Freud (1910d, p. 145)

The analyst's capacity to listen is not established once and for all; it is not sacrosanct or immune to conflicts and compromises. Forces that lie within the analyst as well as those arising in the context of his clinical interaction can readily disturb it. Minor fluctuations in the extent and quality of attunement are frequent and perhaps inevitable; state-related conditions in the analyst (e.g., fatigue, overwork) and impingements of external reality (e.g., loud conversations just outside the office, the building's fire alarm being set off) are often the culprits. The resultant disturbances in listening do affect the analytic work but the problems arising from them are generally transient and correctible. Consequently these do not form the topic of my discourse which focuses upon factors that lead to sustained compromise of the analyst's listening capacity.

Hearing impairment

Any consideration of factors that impede "analytic listening", or for that matter, *any* listening must begin with a statement that is so self-evident as to border on being comical. The first requirement for listening is an intact capacity for hearing. While lapses of hearing due to extraneous noise are excusable, those caused by "internal noise" constitute countertransference resistance and need self-analytic attention, supervision, and consultation with colleagues. The possibility of an actual hearing impairment must also be considered in this context. Not infrequently one comes across analysts with hearing aids though one can never be confident about the efficiency of these devices in the clinical situation. More distressing is the encounter with analysts who do not wear hearing aids but seem to be suffering from mild to moderate hearing loss. This is often politely tolerated by their analytic peers to a much greater extent than a surgical practice group's tolerance would be of a colleague's hand tremors. Some further attention to this matter is clearly needed on the part of various ethics and "impaired analyst" committees of the analytic societies.

Strikingly, there is no mention of this problem in psychoanalytic literature. However, when one extends this search beyond the PEP Web to include PsycINFO (a compendium of over 2.5 million papers, book chapters, reviews, and dissertation abstracts in the field of psychology), Wantuch's (2002) study of clinicians with adult-onset hearing loss does make its way to the computer screen.[1] Based upon psychodynamic interviews with eleven such subjects, the study found that most were in denial about their impairment and its negative impact upon their clinical work. Wantuch's finding can be viewed as the counterpart of what I have asserted above, namely that the colleagues of such clinicians tend to overlook their hearing loss under the guise of civility and good manners. The adverse effects upon listening to patients (e.g., not noticing their low-pitched mumbling, sighs, and sobs) go unrecognised and unreported.[2]

In stating this, I do not ignore the fact that "hearing" and "listening" are not synonymous. Hearing begins in the middle ear and is organised in the auditory cortex. Listening begins somewhere in the temporal cortex. Hearing is a bodily function while listening—to a great extent—is a mental function.[3] "Listening is not done by the ears but by the mind. We hear sounds but we listen to meanings" (Meissner, 2000, p. 319). All this is true but also true is the fact that listening largely depends upon hearing. One can hear without listening. But one cannot listen without hearing (for "listening" to silence, see Chapter Two). In simple words, an intact capacity for hearing is a must for an analyst.

Characterological resistance

Our enthusiastic endorsement of the concept of "analytic identity" (Bacon, 2000; Lhulier, 2005; Rosen, 2000; Skolnikoff, 2000) has the pitfall of minimising the fact that character-wise psychoanalysts are not all the same. In fact, there is perhaps as large a variation in personality attributes among analysts as there is in the general population. Freud was keenly aware of this. He declared that "Analysts are people who have learned to practice a particular art; alongside of this, they may be allowed to be human beings like anyone else" (1937c, p. 247) Three quarters of a century later in a mildly ironical comment upon the writing style of various prominent analysts, I staked out a similar position.

> Hartmann and Jacobson, for instance, write as no-nonsense basic scientists. Winnicott is known for his elusive simplicity. Guntrip comes across as an anguished humanitarian, Khan as an enigmatic (and, later, mad) guru, Brenner as a meticulous surgeon, Kohut as a joyful explorer, Kernberg as an inspired teacher, Limentani as a reassuring internist, and Volkan as an enchanting historian, to name a few. (Akhtar, 1993, p. 519)

The metaphors I used gave voice to my conviction that these psychoanalysts could not represent a characterological monolith; they differed from each other in important ways. Guntrip's (1975) description of his analyses with Fairbairn and Winnicott attests to this by demonstrating the vastly different relating styles on these two analysts' part. Now, this can have (or, shall we say, does have?) implications for analytic listening. In other words, certain themes in the patient's material might be picked up by an analyst with this or that personality attribute and another theme (or set of themes) by one who is characterologically different. Poland (1996) notes that:

> If the analyst has a need to hear selectively, such as if the analyst has the need always to see the patient as an innocent victim,

never to see the patient as aggressive or hateful except in innocent self-defense, then the patient's perceived feeling state will always be a selective facet, never becoming more fully true to the total psychic state of the patient. This is, of course, equally true in the other direction, if the analyst has a preference for matters of aggression and power and is uncomfortable with matters of closeness, intimacy, and love. (1996, pp. 148–149)

Besides such *qualitative* differences in listening caused by variations in analysts' characters, there is the darker possibility of *quantitative* differences in their listening capacity. To be sure, all analysts try to listen carefully to their patients but whether they succeed to an equal extent remains unclear. With the undeniable decline of standards for selection of psychoanalytic trainees (especially in the United States), the resulting concern is no longer a matter of idle speculation. It is a serious issue since a robust listening capacity, honed by principles of theory and technique, is the hallmark of a "good" analyst. Character traits that block this capacity are therefore problematic for clinical work and, in the long run, for the dignity and safety of the profession at large.

Given this, a brief detour in the characterological foundations of the capacity to listen might not be out of place. Now, to my mind, listening is fundamentally a maternal activity. It requires putting one's own concerns aside and cultivating a sense of devotion to the other; Winnicott's (1966) phrase the "ordinary devoted mother" readily comes to mind in this context. Listening requires opening one's heart and mind to someone else and taking in their mental content; the metaphor of a receptive maternal vagina that grasps father's penis is hard to overlook here. Listening requires not being in a hurry to interrupt the narrative, to question, to arrive at conclusions, and to give the material being offered a readily well-polished form. All these qualities, namely, devotion, receptivity, and containing without rushing to "explain", are characteristically maternal, hence feminine (see also Greenson, 1960 in this regard). The well-developed capacity for listening therefore requires characterological comfort with feminine identifications, regardless of one's actual gender.

A related facet of listening is the "ingestion" of someone else's spoken words. Such openness also has the remote echoes of an infant gladly taking in the maternal breast. A good capacity for listening therefore also emanates from comfort with one's orally receptive infantile self-representations. Yet another element in listening is a certain amount of slowing down, an unhurried sort of mentation, or to borrow a phrase from Mahler, Pine, and Bergman (1975), a certain "low keyedness". Absence of internal noise and tolerance of what noise does exist within oneself therefore enhance the capacity of listening. In essence, a good capacity for listening comes from a character organisation that has peacefully assimilated early identifications with a devoted mother, accepted at an archaic but deep level the imago of a receptive maternal vagina, is unafraid of its own baby-on-the-breast self-representation, and does not rely upon "manic defense" (Klein, 1935; Winnicott, 1935) on a habitual basis. Too conflicted (or deficient) maternal identifications, too anxiety-producing infantile self-representations, too intense a denial of maternal sexuality, and too much use of manic defence lead to a characterological style that is unsuited for the act of listening.

Conceptual rigidity

Another variable that can impact upon listening is strict allegiance to one or the other psychoanalytic model. Look at the following examples. An "ego psychologist" sees only the drive-defence sort of compromises in the patient's material. A "Kernbergian" sees idealisation as a defence against regression and a "Kohutian" sees it as a resumption of a thwarted developmental need. A "Mahlerian" regards patients' fluctuating levels of intimacy as representing merger-abandonment anxieties while a "relationist" sees a craftily enacted scenario of mutual teasing and seduction in the same oscillation. A "Kleinian" views patients' hatred of the analyst's silence as an envious attack on a withholding breast while a "Winnicottian" views that very outrage as a manifestation of hope (that the analyst can "survive" the patient's assault) and therefore of love!

Admittedly, these are caricatures. Nonetheless, the point I am trying to make is a serious one: a rigid allegiance to one or the other type of analytic thinking can narrow the way one listens to the patient (see also Hedges, 1983). Worse, it can lead to a situation where the analyst does not listen at all because his theory offers him a prepackaged and formulaic understanding. Let us take the following clinical illustration and see how analysts "committed" to different theoretical models might listen to the patient's communication.

Clinical vignette 28

> Dina Maldonado is a young woman from Peru who has entered psychoanalysis for vague feelings of anxiety and depression, coupled with a sense that she is not realising her academic potential. She has dreams of becoming a clinical psychologist but finds herself performing below par for admission in a good training programme. I suspect she feels guilty underneath it all but the sources of such guilt are unclear to me. It is too early in our work to have clarity in this regard.
>
> One day, I begin the session by letting her know that something has come up because of which I would be unable to meet with her for the first two sessions of the next week. I add that I regret the short notice but find the situation unavoidable. Dina responds by saying, "I understand. These things happen all the time." I wait to see if she will speculate as to what "these things" might be. She does not. She remains quiet for a while and then says, "I do not know why, but I'm thinking of my grandmother. You know, my mother's mother. She was a wonderful woman and I loved her a lot." She pauses and then goes on: "Last year, she passed away. I mean it was not a horrible death or anything like that. She was in her eighties, you know. But I miss her very much."
>
> Dina keeps talking and gradually her mind moves on to intricate details of Peruvian funeral rites. I find myself raptly absorbed, feeling enriched by learning all the cultural details. Returning to a self-observing stance a few moments later, I begin to think about what actually is going on between us.

Allow me, at this point, to leave what I surmised and how I intervened aside. Instead, let me put this snippet of clinical work in front of three imaginary analysts and see how they might listen to it and what might they say about it.

- *A Freudian ego-psychologist*: "What I hear is that the patient responded to the analyst's announcement of cancellation by compliance which warded off the affect stirred up by the news. Perhaps she did not feel safe enough to express her feelings with (and towards) the analyst; he was 'abandoning' her anyway. Her subsequent associations, however, demonstrate that the affect did become conscious by attaching itself to the memory of the departed grandmother and the patient's sadness over it. The talk of funeral rites was then intended to ward off a sadness and to bring the analyst (obviously an immigrant himself) closer to her."

- *A Kleinian*: "The patient responds to the analyst's announcement of a cancellation by thinking of someone who has died. Why? I mean, she could have thought of someone who has left the city for a better job or to be with a lover. No, she thinks of someone who has died. This betrays her murderous impulse towards the analyst. Her subsequent missing the 'grandmother' (the analyst) is a testimony to the inner emptiness that has resulted after her attack on the good internal object. This is followed by a fear (projection, of course) that the analyst will decipher her murderous intent and will retaliate. The cultural bit is a manic defence against the resulting paranoid anxieties."

- *A Winnicottian*: "The patient handles the impingement (i.e., the news of the analyst's cancelling two sessions of the next week) by accommodating the analyst. The politeness is, however, false and leads to a rupture of the continuity of being. Feeling fragmented, the patient resorts to memories (of her grandmother) that can 'hold' her from within; the fact that she does not evoke her mother but thinks of her grandmother makes one wonder about the potential breach in the mother-child relationship and how that might have been evoked by the analyst's cancellation. In any case, because the patient is hurt by the rupture of their (her and her analyst's) continuity, there develops a desperate quality to her seeking refuge in the idealised past. The vigorous turn to culture can thus be seen as a form of masturbation."

To be sure, each of these analysts can be "correct". However, each might be missing what the other two are able to decipher. Since psychological matters are invariably subject to the "principle of multiple determination" (Waelder, 1936), the inherent one-sidedness of their perspectives has the potential of missing something of significance in the patient's material. Let me put it bluntly: any analyst who really listens to his or her patient cannot be rigidly committed to any theoretical model. Genuine respect for all such models without exclusive commitment to any of them is the only assurance that one can truly listen to what the patient is trying to convey. Pine's (1988) cogent reminder that psychoanalysis has "four psychologies" (drive, ego, object relations, and the self) and that each of these demand listening and speaking rights in the clinical arena, must be kept in mind. In other words, the analyst needs to be flexible and open-minded vis-à-vis theory but not entirely devoid of a theory. He might move between theories to accommodate what he is discovering from moment to moment in his clinical work. Aulagnier's (1979) concept of "even suspended theorization" captures best what I am trying to say here.

Baranger also notes that while rigid commitment to one particular theory can lead to becoming deaf to the patient's communications, having no theory is hardly advisable (or possible).

> The analyst must steer a course between two contrasting dangers: the forced application of a pre-existing theory, which will ultimately lead to spurious interpretations, and the whole complex of chaotic theories. The analyst's scheme of reference is what guides both the search for the point of urgency and the formulation of the interpretation. This scheme of reference is the quintessence, condensed and worked out personally by each analyst, of his theoretical allegiances, his knowledge of the analytic literature, his clinical experience—especially his failures—what he has been able to learn about himself in his analysis, and his identifications with his analyst and supervisors—as well as the theoretical fashions that periodically sweep through the psychoanalytic movement. The degree of coherence and elaboration of these different influences varies considerably from analyst to analyst. (2009, p. 96)

To be sure, the analyst's scheme of reference should not become ossified; it must be guided by knowledge of the patient's history as well as memory of the analytic process as it has unfolded up to the moment under consideration.

Countertransference blocks

Also of note in this context is Freud's grim warning that "no psychoanalyst goes further than his own complexes and resistances permit" (1910d, p. 145), which highlights how personal problems on the other side of the couch can impede proper listening and intervening. Racker (1968) went on to distinguish two types of countertransference blocks to the receptivity of the analyst. "Concordant countertransference" responses are those in which the analyst identifies with the patient's own central feeling state. "Complementary countertransferences" result from the analyst's identification with a significant object that is projected into him by the patient. In the former, the analyst identifies with the patient's self-representation and in the latter with the patient's object representation. While partial and transient identifications of this sort can help develop empathy for the patient's inner experience, unquestioned and total identifications in this regard make listening peacefully to the patient difficult. Take, for instance, the following clinical example.[4]

Clinical vignette 29

Pamela Kasinetz, an elderly woman of extreme wealth, sought psychotherapy for depression and anxiety of recent origin. The apparent trigger for this was the worsening relationship with her husband of more than three decades. With their children no longer at home, the two had become quite alienated; he was engrossed in his business and she with her social commitments and philanthropic work. Matters became worse when Pamela ran into an "adorable" seven- to eight-year-old Cambodian boy in a shopping mall and "fell in love with him". She took it upon herself to help him and his financially strained family. The boy gradually became her constant companion. Paying huge sums of money to his parents, Pamela pretty much took over his life. She would pick him up from school, bring him home, shower him with lavish gifts, and indulge all his whims and desires; his friends also were welcome at her house and were treated with similar indulgence. While numerous examples can be given, one instance should suffice where she spent in excess of thirty thousand dollars over a weekend entertaining her little "friend" and his four playmates. All this led to frequent arguments between Pamela and her husband who insisted on putting limits on her expenses.

Seeking symptomatic relief, Pamela appeared unprepared to look into the deeper meanings of her fascination with this little boy. Raised in a family of means, she readily dismissed any enquiry into a childhood sense of feeling deprived and thus blocked the therapist's efforts at linking her runaway altruism with potential unconscious issues pertaining to early trauma. It was all "real" and rationalised in terms of kindness and generosity towards the underprivileged, as far as she was concerned. Soon after starting treatment, she expressed a desire to pay a much greater fee for her sessions, quoting what appeared to be truly an exorbitant amount. The situation was complicated by parallel problems in the therapist's countertransference to her and to the financial glitter of the situation. Having suffered a childhood parental loss at about the same age as the Cambodian boy Pamela so adored, and being financially strapped himself because of a recent personal crisis, the therapist was made terribly uncomfortable by Pamela's financial seductions. Reacting defensively, he not only made premature transference interpretations but also sternly rejected her offers. He failed to explicate and explore them in a peaceful manner. Pamela soon dropped out of treatment.

This adverse outcome seems to have been the result of a number of factors: (i) the therapist's current financial distress made it hard for him to listen peacefully to his patient's extravagance: it stirred up too much greed; (ii) his childhood trauma made it difficult for him to hear about his patient's indulgence in a little boy: it stirred up too much envy; and (iii) not seeking a consultation in what was obviously a difficult clinical situation for him, it led to defensive recoil and over-interpretation. Flying solo under these circumstances was an inappropriate clinical choice. And yet the vignette has didactic value. It reveals some important variables in pre-empting, precluding, or gainfully using these emergent countertransference feelings, including the therapist's (i) inner "good objects" (Klein, 1935, 1940), the presence of which will diminish his vulnerability to greed and envy; (ii) an aptitude and skill for learning from his subjective experiences in the course of treatment, and (iii) a willingness to seek outside consultation in difficult clinical situations. The reason for mentioning these well-established observations is to balance the current enthusiasm about the informative potential of countertransference since that seems to have eclipsed the fact that countertransference can also impede listening.

Such compromise of analytic attention at times becomes discernible only in retrospect. This is especially the case when the patient's chain of associations is found to be truly engaging by the analyst. Here is an example of a patient's discourse of this sort.

Clinical vignette 30

"You know, Doc, this sex thing is beyond me. It just does not make any sense. Think about it. What is a man trying to do when he is having sex with a woman? I mean, if he is trying to get inside her, sex is not really the way. Because in sex, one just goes a few inches in, then pulls oneself out deliberately to thrust again but you know what? One can't go any more deep than before. One just goes on and on but never really gets fully inside her. And then one ejaculates and comes out all shrivelled up. One is hardly a man now. Not able to get inside her at all!

"You know what is a better way to get inside a woman. Let her be pregnant with you. Now you are all the way in. She walks, talks, goes to work, reads the newspaper—no matter what, you are inside her. I mean, she eats, sleeps, takes a shower, even makes love to her man—whatever—but you are snugly in there. And then after months when you come out, it is not a moment of shrivelled humiliation. It is a moment of great joy and celebration. Everyone is happy. The woman is beaming. People kiss you and shower you with gifts.

"Let me put it bluntly, Doc, you hold my hand and let us go for a walk. You,—yes, you, because you are a smart guy, you spot a beautiful woman and I assure you that I'd rather be her son than her husband."

Listening to this chain of associations, I found myself so raptly absorbed and so admiring of my patient's eloquence that, for a few moments, I paid little attention to the multifaceted themes contained in it. Mesmerised by the literary quality of his speech, I failed to note the libidinised enactment that was taking place right then and there between us. By putting me in charge of selecting the "most beautiful woman" (i.e., mother) and by choosing to be her son, my patient was surrendering his Oedipal competitiveness. However, by being inside her longer than the man (me/father) who has sex with her, he was mocking and defeating me. And, by offering me a lullaby-like recitation, he had moved both of us out of the sexual realm. Yet there were unmistakable negative Oedipal undercurrents in the "love" that was developing between us as the tale unfolded. All this is true but my main point is that the graceful and sonorous quality of his speech led to a downward shift in the acuity of my psychoanalytic attention.[5] In other words, a countertransference reaction temporarily impaired my listening capacity.

Cultural differences

Listening can also be affected by cultural difference within the clinical dyad. Matters of nationality, social class, race, ethnicity, aesthetic preferences, and politics can have considerable impact upon the empathy and attunement of the analyst (Abbasi, 2008; Akhtar, 1999, 2011; Gorkin, 1996; Roland, 1996). Subtle, or not too subtle, prejudices on the analyst's part can become mobilised when differences along these dimensions exist and preclude a stance of neutrality vis-à-vis the patient's material. Far from being matters of expressive idiom and unobjectionable aspects of lifestyle, the value system of the dyad affects the clinical exchange in significant, if subtle, ways.

> [The patient's value system] and ideals may take forms compatible or incompatible with the ideals of individual analysts: propensities toward austerity or luxury, toward the acceptance or non-acceptance of commonly held standards of choice of work, or even of dress, which may be treated by one psychoanalyst as symptoms and by another with toleration. (Klauber, 1968, p. 131)

Values of the sort that can affect listening are the product of the socio-economic status, parental dictates and lifestyles, the era and nation in which one has been raised and is practising, educational institutions attended, and superego modification via extra-familial identifications during late adolescence and early adulthood. Take a look at the following situation.

Clinical vignette 31

> Pradip Bhandari, a recent medical graduate from India and now a psychiatric resident physician, begins his session of analysis by saying that he would not be able to come for one of his sessions next week. There is something else he must do. As the analyst remains quiet, Pradip explains that his wife's brother is getting engaged and

the uncle and aunt of his wife are coming from Bombay to attend the ceremony; he has to pick them up from JFK Airport in New York. The trip would take pretty much the whole day and that is why he is not asking for an alternative time for that day's session. Pradip's North American analyst finds himself wondering about this arrangement and asks how it is that he got chosen for this task? Did he volunteer for it? It turns out that Pradip's physician wife could not go because she is "on call" that day and the relatives coming from India have never been abroad and would certainly need help. They had to be picked up and there was no one else but Pradip to do the task.

If the analyst views such a patient's missing a session as solely (or even mainly) a resistance, something important in the patient's ethos would be missed. The analyst would have failed to "listen" to the cultural ego ideal and some widely accepted ways of being that are integral to his patient's inner world. Putting this in the background of his patient's near-perfect attendance and his giving a fairly advanced notice for missing a session makes one grasp the essential "physiology" of this material. Peacefully accepting it would strengthen the therapeutic alliance while regarding it as resistance would result in an iatrogenic "pathology". Misattunement to cultural nuances can thus compromise analytic listening.

Religion also plays a role here. If, for instance, the analyst is indifferent or hostile to religion, he is likely to be highly sceptical towards his analysand's spiritual yearnings (e.g., Griefinger, 1997). He may sidestep such issues, subtly devalue them, or quickly reduce them to their alleged instinctual origins. On the other hand, if the analyst is religious, his attitude towards such associations is likely to be more tolerate and permissive (e.g., Rizzuto, 2001).

A dramatic illustration of such attitudes comes from the 31 st Annual Margaret Mahler Symposium held on May 6, 2000, in Philadelphia, PA. Published proceedings of the event (Akhtar & Parens, 2001) reveal the sharp divergence between the renowned Jesuit analyst, William Meissner, and an avowedly atheist psychiatrist, James Anderson Thomson, Jr.

Meissner (2001) presented the case of Martha, a tall woman in her sixties who "wore printed dresses down to the ankles, lace collars, straw hats with a flower on them—looking something out of a Dickens novel" (p. 112). The only daughter of her parents, Martha had grown up with four brothers. She had got along well with them as she did with her mostly male fellow workers at her current job. She had never dated and was a virgin. Her problem revolved around obscene thoughts and images that came to her while attending mass or during her prayers. She felt enormous guilt about having such thoughts. Meissner concluded the following:

> The erotic character of these intrusive thoughts and images, I thought, was entirely consistent with her rather obsessional character structure. My early impression was that her extreme religiosity and her obsessional defenses were serving as a barrier against unresolved sexual conflicts and that these had probably been a source of conflict and distress for most of her life. (p. 113)

As the treatment unfolded, Martha revealed that some time ago, she too had sought pastoral counselling for similar anxieties and that her work with that pastor had led to his fondling her, often with her in the nude. However, any attempt on Meissner's part to bring her attention to her having been "abused" led Martha to "become quickly upset and agitated, her voice trembling and her speech impaired" (p. 115). Meissner concluded that this approach was not going to work. He felt stuck, searched his mind for "any scraps of psychoanalytic lore that might help. But I kept running into dead ends" (p. 115). He concluded that the only common ground on which he and his patient could understand each other was the Catholic tradition. Meissner recounts his next step:

> One day when she was recounting one of her agonizing episodes of intrusive sexual thoughts, I inquired "Martha, do you know what a temptation is?" She stopped and looked at me for a minute, as though I had suddenly stopped speaking Swahili and started to speak a language she understood. I went on to explain that when the devil wanted to tempt good souls who were living a good life, his tactic was to cause them to be distressed or disturbed, and that he used whatever device he could get his hands on to pull it off, to interfere with their good works, or with their tranquility of soul. Might it be that she was such a case, I wondered? If old Satan could toss a rock through a window of her peace of soul, he would have

scored a victory. Her reaction was interesting. When I mentioned the devil, her eyes lit up. We had identified the enemy, the cause of all the trouble …. My comment had given the problem a local habitation and a name. What had been disturbing, confusing, and incomprehensible to her before was now relocated in a context that was familiar, comprehensible, and therefore manageable. (Ibid., pp. 116–117)

James Anderson Thomson, Jr, the discussant of Meissner's paper, bristled at this. He questioned the gaps in Meissner's report of the patient's history but his sharpest criticism was reserved for the shift in Meissner's listening (hence, intervening) that occurred in response to Martha's guilt over thoughts about the sexual orgasms of Jesus on the cross. Thomson's retort against Meissner's describing the relief his patient felt upon being told that Satan was responsible for such thoughts sums it up well.

Meissner clearly believes that "She believed in the devil and knew exactly what I was talking about. My comment had located the problem, which had been disturbing, confusing, and incomprehensible to her before, and relocated it in a context that was familiar, comprehensible, and therefore manageable." If a patient is delusional and believes that she is the Queen of England, certainly if we addressed her as Her Royal Highness that would make her relieved and her eyes might light up. Does that make it right? (2001, p. 145)

This is the stuff of courtroom drama. However, even under less dramatic circumstances, matters involving abortion, homosexuality, impending death, and life after death, especially tend to evoke countertransference reactions that are, at least in part, governed by the analyst's religious beliefs. The specific religion to which the analyst belongs can also come to play an important, even if subtle, role in his listening to the patient's sociopolitical views.[6] Consider the following situations.

- A Hindu surgeon reports that he bows his head to the elephant-headed deity, *Ganesha*, that sits on his office desk before walking towards the operating theatre. He claims that if he forgets to do so, the surgery is botched.

- A Jewish lawyer declares that Muslims are basically primitive and praises Israel for the assassination of Hamas leaders. He firmly believes that the land of Israel was given to Jews by God.
- A Lutheran college student struggles with difficulty in finding boyfriends and potential marital partners due to her religiously-based refusal to have premarital sex. She wishes to have a long period of dating before engagement and marriage but one that would not involve having sexual intercourse.
- A Muslim analysand expresses his outrage at the recent newspaper cartoons ridiculing the Prophet Mohammed; he says that the murder of Theo van Gogh, the Dutch documentary maker, was a legitimate retribution for his mockery of Muslim customs.

Now ask yourself whether religious and non-religious Jewish, Christian, Hindu, and Muslim analysts would listen to these associations in exactly the same manner? As much as we would like to believe they would, the doubt that this might not be the case nags at our theoretical conscience. We would like to believe that the religious backgrounds of these analysts would not preclude their receiving this material with equanimity and that they would all attend similarly to the surface as well as to the in-depth and symbolic aspects of these communications, especially as they pertain to transference-countertransference developments. However, this view may be idealistic. It overlooks the fact that countertransference experiences in such situations become quite vulnerable to the tricks of "shared ethnic scotoma" (Shapiro & Pinsker, 1973), "acculturation gaps" (Prathikanti, 1997), "excessive culturalization of the analytic ego" (Akhtar, 1999), and "nostalgic collusions" (Akhtar, 2006).

Lest this give the impression that such lapses of analytic attention occur only in cross-cultural clinical work, I hasten to add that homoethnic dyads have their own pitfalls (Akhtar, 2011a). All sorts of countertransference-based "deaf spots" can develop:

> ... especially when the therapist identifies closely with the patient's experiences. The therapist may be more tolerant and less confrontational about some instances of acting out. When this identification is strong, the therapist is often tempted to go the extra mile for the patient ... it is a temptation to reach out to such patients, in the

sense of being somewhat more didactic and helpful about the process itself. (Tang & Gardner, 1999, p. 16)

Long before Tang and Gardner's comments and talking more specifically regarding psychoanalysis, Boyer had made the following observation.

> Many analysts hold that their work with patients who stem from sociocultural backgrounds similar to their own is more effective than that done with patients from different backgrounds. I am of the opinion that more thorough analyses may result from the treatment of people from the second group, because of the presence of few mutually accepted givens, the defensive and symbolic meanings of which may go uninvestigated. (1979, p. 364)

To be sure, this does not have to happen, but the fact is that it *can* happen. And that is the point—namely, that the cultural and religious background of the analyst (and the sociopolitical stances consequent upon it) *can* come into play under certain circumstances and alter the pathways of empathy and interpretation.

Language problems

These are most clearly evident in the treatment of bilingual patients (Amati-Mehler, Argentieri & Canestri, 1993). Denotations, connotations, aphorisms, colloquialisms, proverbs, curse words, and terms of endearment as well as the mere prosodic qualities of language, all enter into how one speaks and how one's spoken words are received and processed by the listener. While the impact of the patient's bilingualism has received attention, it is only recently that the analyst's bilingualism and its impact on his listening and intervening activities have been raised for consideration (Akhtar, 2006).

Let us take the patient's difficulties with language first. A bilingual patient often finds it hard to convey his subjective experience to the analyst. His vocabulary in their common language is often less extensive than in his mother tongue. His pauses, fumbling for words, and awkward phraseology might lead the analyst to discern meaning where none exists or, more frequently, meaning that does not accord with the patient's intent.

Clinical vignette 32

Professor Miguel Castro was in the second year of a four-day-a-week analysis. He had been struggling for several weeks with angry feelings about an upcoming visit from his mother who lived most of the year in Colombia. His parents divorced when he was two years old and he had been left in the care of an elderly and ailing aunt. She was devoted to him but for as long as he could remember he had lived in fear that she would die and he would be alone in a big house, with nobody to take care of him.

During his adult life Professor Castro's mother had assuaged her guilt about leaving him as a child by lavishing gifts and money on him, much to the chagrin of her current husband. His mother had forewarned him that she had been placed on a strict budget for this particular trip and could not risk her precarious marriage by indulging him in her usual manner. When he was a child his mother's infrequent visits had been associated with the extravagant gifts she brought him. Even in adulthood, he expected them as compensation for her inability to give him love. During moments of intense affect, Professor Castro lapsed into Spanish to express his rage and ill wishes towards his mother. He feared I would be shocked by the magnitude of his hate and by the sadistic fantasies he had about torturing his mother till she begged his forgiveness for abandoning him as a child. Use of his mother tongue also provided him with a way to expose my "bourgeois" ignorance, as he put it. He was fluent in four languages; I knew only one.

For the week before his mother's arrival Professor Castro had been muttering in Spanish, at times hissing through his teeth that he was in no mood to have "that woman" in his home. She had telephoned to tell him that she had been diagnosed with a mild cardiac condition and she was worried that the long flight would make it worse. He feared that she would become ill and he would have to take care of her. He wondered if now that she was *"a las puertas de la muerte"* (at death's door), she would finally realise what a bad mother she had been. Towards the end of the third session of the week he seemed to be calming down a little. I thought I picked up the words *"santa"* (saint) and then *"buena"* (good) in an utterance about his mother. I commented on his shift in attitude towards her and wondered what had brought this about. He was silent for several minutes then accused me of being sarcastic. It came out that in fact he had said the word "*sana*", meaning rage and then "*bueno*" in relation to himself. He was feeling good about the rage he felt towards his mother.

In the session after this, Professor Castro unleashed a vitriolic attack on the American education system, its "bourgeois" narrow-mindedness. He was fluent in four languages. His colleagues at his university knew only English but were so stupid that they did not always understand his accent. I commented that I, too, knew only English and that my foolish attempts to understand Spanish the day before had made him very angry. He turned around and said with contempt, "You should stick to what you know." Over the next few weeks I came to understand how important it was to him to have power over what I could know about him. Above all, he did not want me to know that underneath his rage towards his mother was the desperate longing of a little boy to be loved by her.

This clinical vignette, lent to me by a colleague, demonstrates that transient compromises of the analyst's listening can bring out transference-based fantasies from the patient and thus facilitate treatment. Becoming more frequent and left "undiagnosed", the analyst's misunderstandings due to the patient's difficulty with language can, however, become problematic.

The realm of bodily functions and especially sexuality is most vulnerable to getting caught up in such a conundrum. A bilingual patient, for instance, might talk with ease in his acquired language about sexual intercourse, fellatio, and cunnilingus or, for that matter, about defecation, urination, and farting, and appear "resistance-free" to the analyst. However, the same patient might experience great anxiety and shame in uttering corresponding words in his mother tongue (Akhtar, 1999; Amati-Mahler, Argentieri & Canestri, 1993; Ferenczi, 1911). An analyst who is content with listening to his patient in their common language might miss such affects, their origins, and their transferential basis. [7]

The analyst's own bilingualism mostly involves his interventional activities (Akhtar, 1999, 2011) but can also impact upon his listening.

Clinical vignette 33

> In one of her turmoil-ridden analyses, Josephine Heller, a forty-year-old research scientist, tells me of a ruthless and rather cruel berating by her husband. The details she lays out are chilling. However, it is when she ruefully adds that once he seemed certain of having devastated her, he started to act very gentle and kind towards her. She could, however, discern the patronising contempt in such "love". As she was talking, I found myself inwardly repeating a line from Ghalib, the nineteenth century doyen of Urdu poetry: *"ki mere qatal ke baad, us ne jafaa sey toba"* (literally: after killing me, he decided to renounce cruelty forever). My "listening" to her, not in our shared English language, but in my mother tongue, Urdu, signals that something usually deep is at work between us. After all, it is only four to five times a year that I "listen" to my English-speaking patients in Urdu.

A bilingual analyst is thus signalled by his unconscious of the stirrings of transference-countertransference phenomena hitherto unnoticed. Needless to add that the analyst's bilingualism does not always have such positive effect; it can also contribute to the analyst's missing the nuances and subtleties of his "native" patients' language.

Concluding remarks

In this chapter, I have delineated six variables that have the potential of impeding psychoanalytic listening. These include (i) hearing impairment, (ii) characterological resistance on the analyst's part, (iii) countertransference blocks, (iv) conceptual rigidity and an unshakeable commitment to this or that theoretical model, (v) marked sociocultural difference between the analyst and the patient, and (vi) bilingualism of one or both parties in the therapeutic dyad. The list is perhaps not exhaustive and the variables mentioned here are hardly exclusive of each other. More than one can exist simultaneously and one variable (e.g., conceptual rigidity) can be affected by another (e.g., countertransference blocks). Some factors (e.g., mild hearing loss) might be remediable while others (e.g., cultural difference) are there to stay. One must therefore become and remain aware of the potentially deleterious impact of these factors upon analytic listening. I have sought to make such impact vivid and convincing by bringing forward corroborative evidence from earlier literature and by offering suggestive clinical vignettes from my practice.

The main point I have tried to underscore is that the analyst's listening capacity is vulnerable to compromise and therefore needs guarding and vigilant attention. Ongoing and scrupulous self-analysis helps in this regard. At times, however, such attention can only come as a result of making presentations to a peer group. "Writing openly" (Coen, 2002) about cases also offers an opportunity to think things through and take a fresh look at the material.

Another avenue to "freshen up" one's listening capacity vis-à-vis a given analysand is to read one's notes of the initial consultation with him or her. A paradox awaits here. On the one hand, we analysts put premium upon the "deeper", transference-based information as it emerges during the course of treatment and are therefore inclined to put aside our early impressions and the patient's first recounting of his or her history. On the other hand, looking up the notes taken during (or immediately after) the first consultation can jog one's memory about things mentioned there but never brought up during the subsequent clinical work. One might even question whether those things did surface but in disguised forms that went unnoticed. The dark possibility that one had not been listening properly to the patient can become evident as a result. In sum, reading about the patient's psychopathology and cultural background, self-analysis, peer group input, writing about clinical material, and re-visiting early notes constitute prophylactic measures against the deterioration of the analyst's listening capacity.

Notes

1. I am grateful to Dr Leon Hoffman who, on May 10, 2011, posted this information on the open communication line for the members of the American Psychoanalytic Association.
2. Another problem is posed by the sleepiness and fatigue of elderly psychoanalysts who continue to have a packed clinical schedule and tend to get drowsy towards the afternoon (Kaspars Tuters, personal communication, March 9, 2012).
3. See Chapters Three and Four for passages considering the enlistment of our bodily selves in the process of listening.
4. I am grateful to a colleague (who prefers to remain anonymous) for lending me this clinical material.

5. My affective involvement in this instance clearly exceeded the bounds of "unobjectionable positive counter-transference" (Fox, 1998). The latter is not only inevitable but necessary to sustain the analyst's participation in the long and tedious task of analysis. Its "silent" presence is unmasked when the analyst presents clinical material to peers. Almost invariably, they find the patient "sicker". This is largely due to their not having access to the visual and auditory cues and, more important, the warmth of familiarity that develops in the clinical dyad over months and years.

6. Political beliefs of the analyst and the analysand perhaps constitute the "last taboo" in psychoanalysis. The fact is that the profession is rife with subterranean but powerful political leanings. This is most marked in the organisational realm; the three regions of the International Psychoanalytic Association, for instance, are North America, Latin America, and Europe, leaving out a large segment of the world, namely, Africa, Asia, and Australia. Psychoanalytic societies in the latter regions are subsumed under one of the three recognised regions. The results are geoculturally astounding: China, Japan, and Korea are under North America; Australia, Israel, and India under Europe. As if this were not enough, the literature of our field shows its own biases. Some prejudices draw attention, others do not. Within the United States itself, psychoanalysis has almost completely ignored the African American population. Many such examples can be given, but the essential point is that psychoanalysis is hardly "politics free" and needs to wake up to this. The recent books by Frosh (1999), Layton, Hollander, and Gutwill (2006), Hollander (2010), and Bosteels (2012) are therefore a highly welcome addition to our literature.

7. Bilingual patients are not unique in deploying "safer" speech patterns in the service of resistance. Defensive preference for a sanitised language (e.g., "oral sex" instead of "blow job") can also be witnessed in monolingual patients.

CHAPTER SIX

Refusing to listen

"Psychoanalysis is justly suspicious. One of its rules is that whatever interrupts the progress of analytic work is a resistance."

—Sigmund Freud (1900a, p. 517)

Spring 1978. I am a junior faculty member in the Department of Psychiatry of the University of Virginia's School of Medicine. I am considering psychoanalytic training and want to apply to an analytic institute. But I am hesitant. Real and imagined burdens of time and money are not what bother me. I am fearful of rejection, entertaining all sorts of scenarios in which the institute will refuse me entry. Feeling stuck, I seek the counsel of Dan Josephthal, who is a supervisor of mine. He is a warm man with a radiant smile and a twinkle in his eyes. He is solidly grounded in reality and unpretentious. There is also a matter-of-fact sort of tenderness about him. In short, he is a *mensch*.

We arrive at an Italian restaurant near his office the next day. After we have placed our orders and exchanged a few pleasantries, he looks at me keenly and says, "Tell me why would you *not* apply for analytic training?" I mumble something to the effect that I fear I might be rejected. He seems puzzled and asks me, "Why?" As I open my mouth to reply, he raises his hand indicating me to stop and says, "I am not interested in listening to those kinds of reasons." His warmth and friendliness tell me that his shutting me up is not from rudeness. It is actually an act of fatherly tenderness, a nudge to momentarily pull me out of my silly neurotic inhibitions. I get the point he is making. By refusing to listen to (what he rightly anticipated to be) my misplaced self-castigation, he cleaves my ego into an experiencing and an observing section. In effect, he makes an interpretation, telling me that I should not allow my neurotic anxieties to come in the way of my academic growth. Two days later, I mail my application to the psychoanalytic institute.

The memory of this encounter remains with me. I return to think about it off and on. Such self-analytic work leads to a far deeper understanding of what actually took place then, what I had wanted from my supervisor, and how many meanings were embedded in his deft gesture. Gradually, the whole episode changes its status from a Zen *koan* to a cherished poem. I think I am more or less done with it. Little do I know that the topic of refusing to listen to certain kinds of material would pop up in my clinical writings thirty-four years later.

Speaking as an impediment to treatment

In subscribing to the "fundamental rule" (Freud, 1900a) of psychoanalysis, the injunction for the patient to free-associate, we overlook that the intended enhancement of communication might not occur in each such instance. Instead, the patient's talking might acquire functions other than that of information transfer; it might begin to serve defensive aims or become a vehicle of instinctual discharge. Breuer and Freud's (1895d) suggestion that, under the influences of regression, the aural "word representations" typical of "Systems Conscious and Preconscious" can turn back into tactile thing representations typical of the "System Unconscious" is pertinent in this context. Transformed into their concrete and sensual counterparts, spoken words can then become instruments of acting upon the object world. Ferenczi's (1911) astute observation that obscene words in a mother tongue possess a much greater discharge value (hence, stricter moral prohibition) than those in a later acquired language has conceptual proximity to Freud's point; in the mother tongue, such words are close to the "thing representation" since the child has a limited vocabulary and knows only one word for the body part or action in question.

A major exponent of these ideas was Ella Freeman Sharpe (1940) who noted that words, at their base, reflect natural noises (e.g., hiss, blast) and/or crystallised sounds that emerged in primitive civilisation and denote man's relationship to fellow man, to his environment, to his self-preservation, and to his procreative potential. More importantly, Sharpe unmasked the fact that instinctual aims often seek discharge via the act of speaking. She stated that:

> The discharge of feeling tension, when this is no longer relieved by physical discharge, can take place through speech. The activity of speaking is substituted for the physical activity now restricted at other openings of the body, while words themselves become the very substitutes for the bodily substances. (p. 157)

Applying this to the clinical situation, Reik (1968) talked of the "meaningless speech" (p. 182) of obsessionally ruminating individuals, and Bach (1977) spoke of self-esteem regulating the chatter of narcissistic patients. The incessant talking of certain other patients reflects a desire for seamless merger with the analyst-mother. They talk without any regard for the listener's feelings. Such use of people as containers results in their exploitation rather than exchange with them. The "drug-like use of others as players in one's secret scenarios is founded upon one postulate of the Impossible, namely, that others exist only as part of ourselves" (McDougall, 1985, p. 10).

Fascinatingly, long before these contributors (e.g., Sharpe, Reik, Bach, and McDougall), Ferenczi (1915) had written a paper titled, "Talkativeness" which points out how speaking a lot during sessions can actually derail free association and serve as resistance to analysis. In a built-in irony, Ferenczi's paper is all of two sentences long and is quoted below in its entirety.

> With several patients, talkativeness proved to be a method of resistance. They discussed all considerable immaterial matters superficially in order not to have to speak or reflect on a few important ones. (p. 252)

Ferenczi's emphasis on defensive aims needs to be integrated with the later authors' focus on discharge functions of volubility. The presence of the latter is unmistakable in so-called dirty talk, whereby the subject draws sexual pleasure by using lewd expressions and vivid details of erotic acts in his language. That such "corruption" of language in the clinical situation should not be left unchallenged is what brings us full circle back to the analyst's "refusal to listen".

An unusual technical intervention

A provocative but serious and hitherto unexplored technical possibility[1] pertains to the analyst's letting the patient know that he (or she) refuses to listen to the patient's material. The mere mention of such intervention is sure to horrify most, if not all, psychoanalysts. Therefore, let me quickly explain what I mean by this innovation, under what circumstances it might be indicated, and what is the theoretical rationale and technical yield of it.

Based upon my reading of psychoanalytic literature and over three decades of clinical experience, I have found four indications for the intervention that, for economy of space and time, might be called RTL ("refusal to listen"). These are: (i) RTL for precluding a perverse alliance from the start, (ii) RTL for showing that the endless repetition of an agreed-upon theme hides the search for a certain kind of transference relationship, in effect; (iii) RTL for "spoiling" the perverse pleasure of instinctual discharge via the function of language, and (iv) RTL for the mutually recognised ironical aim of demonstrating that last minute regressions during the termination phase need to be "pushed upward" in the direction of health rather than "pulled back" into analytic deconstruction. These four indications for RTL are now taken up at some length separately.

RTL for precluding a perverse alliance from the start

Establishing and safeguarding the therapeutic frame becomes important from the very beginning of contact with patients. Kernberg's (1984) delineation of "structural interview" demonstrates this point clearly; the patient's inability and/or refusal to follow the step-by-step process necessitate not only investigation but, at times, confrontation and blocking. Writing about this manner of working twenty years ago, I made the following observations:

> An important task during the initial interview, besides collecting information, is to establish, maintain, and safeguard the therapeutic

framework. A patient's naïveté and/or psycho-pathology often exert a pull on the interviewer's work ego in this regard. No hard and fast rule exists for dealing with complex situations that may unexpectedly arise during an initial evaluation. However, a useful guideline is that a temporary giving up of one's neutral stance is almost always preferable over risking harm to the patient or oneself, carrying on an interview under bizarre circumstances, and colluding with someone's pathological agenda. (Akhtar, 1992, p. 289)

An especially tricky situation is when a patient refuses to give identifying information about himself or herself but insists upon talking about the problems needing help. It is in this context that the analyst might be forced to use RTL as an intervention; to eschew its use runs the risk of establishing a perverse alliance and an "everything goes" sort of laissez-faire clinical stance.

Clinical vignette 34

"Julie Robinson" made an appointment to see me for help with some "emotional problems". When we met, though, she refused to give me her address and other identifying information. I asked her reasons for such secrecy. She said that she works as a live-in housekeeper for an extremely wealthy and eccentric man who does not want her to tell anyone that she lives there. She could not give me her street address, therefore; all she could tell me is that she lived in such-and-such a part of the city. As if to buttress the validity of her secretive stance, Julie now revealed that she had given me a false name for herself. Her name was actually Christine Thomson. As if nothing extraordinary had transpired between us, she proceeded to talk about the problems (e.g., insomnia, feelings of anxiety) for which she was seeking help from me. I interrupted her and pointed out that there was a contradiction in her not trusting me with her address or phone number and her readiness to reveal her personal concerns to me. How did she account for that, I asked. She responded by saying, "Alright, I will give you my phone number" and then proceeded to do so. Now, as it happened, I immediately recognised that the phone number did belong to an area of the city that was miles and miles away from wherever she supposedly lived. I put down my writing pad, looked at her, and confronted her with giving me false information. She apologised profusely and suggested that we begin all over again. This time, she would be totally honest with me. Now she told me that even Christine was not her real name. Her real name was Catherine James, she lived at such-and-such a street, and her real phone number was such-and-such. However, in light of the many lies she had spoken thus far, I had little reason to trust her, even though I very much wanted to: how else would I be able to understand and help her? I therefore decided to take a firm stance and check things out for myself. I asked her to open her purse, take out her driver's licence (which would have her *real* name and address) and show it to me. The patient instead went on to talk about how she is unable to sleep and how she feels anxiety all the time. I told her that I was not interested in listening to these issues (i.e., used RTL) unless she showed me her driver's licence. She blushed, became flustered, and refused to do so. As this refusal grew tenacious, I became convinced that she was still not being honest with me. I felt that there was little point in continuing the interview. Using RTL, I indicated to her that I would be glad to see her in the future when she would seek me out with the intention of being honest. And, at this point, I terminated the interview.

Although the patient did not return, this does not necessarily mean that she was "lost" to treatment. She might have learned something of significance from this encounter and might have behaved honestly while seeking help from another therapist. My technical stance consisted of maintaining curiosity, showing flexibility, requiring a basic modicum of honesty, confronting pathological defences, and appealing to the healthy parts of her mind. My RTL was a means of last resort. Conducting the interview in the face of outright lies would have been of little use since all information would have remained suspect.

In all fairness, it should be acknowledged that the patient's superego pathology was not the only contributor to what transpired. The encounter occurred more than twenty years ago when I was far less experienced. Now I hardly ever use RTL during an initial evaluation and on the rare occasions that I do, it is gentle and meant to protect the patient's mental contents from spilling all over the place; the aim is to keep matters at least somewhat coherent so that one can arrive at a mutual understanding of the problem at hand. Whether this "milder" stance would withstand an encounter with a patient of similarly severe superego pathology remains to be seen.

RTL to unmask the sought-after transference relationship

The next indication for refusing to listen is when the patient is repeating something *ad nauseam*. This might include angry complaints about childhood mistreatment by parents, dissatisfaction in a marriage, or a sense that one is being dealt with unfairly at the place of employment. Regardless of the content, the material is repeated over and over again and on each occasion as if it were being reported for the first time. At times, there is a quality of feigned disbelief in the patient who begins complaining with a "Can-you-believe-it?" intonation. The analyst who has heard the complaint hundreds of times before feels burdened and impatient. He wishes to put an end to this litany, and refuses to hear the patient tell the all-too-familiar story once again.

Before going any further let me add something important here. I am fully aware that prominent among the constituents of the analytic attitude are not only a non-judgmental "benevolent neutrality" (Stone, 1961) and the trio of survival, vision, and faith (Akhtar, 2009), but also a resolutely unhurried stance. The analyst must have patience. He listens to the material offered by the patient again and again, each time with a slightly different vantage point and each time grasping a fresh nuance of what the patient is trying to convey. The process is slow and cannot be rushed. This is especially true in the case of patients who suffer from a "basic fault" (Balint, 1968), harbour tenacious "someday ..." and "if only ..." fantasies (Akhtar, 1996), and have been severely traumatised during their childhood. Such patients carry a desperate hope of being understood and helped, though often their expectations are somewhat magical (McDougall, 1985). Nonetheless, before their excessive hope is frustrated either directly or by way of interpretation,

> [T]he patient ought to experience for a sufficient length of time and at different levels the soundness of the therapeutic rapport, the security of being understood, the benefit of a careful and thorough working through of the transference, and a relational structure that enables him or her to contain the comprehension and the elaboration of the disruption of the transference play. (Amati-Mehler & Argentieri, 1989, p. 303)

Considerations of actual time are involved here. For instance, when a patient endlessly laments the loss of a loved one or a bad marriage or a frustrating job situation, it is better, for a long while, to "agree" with the patient and to demonstrate one's understanding of the nature and conscious sources of the patient's agony. Balint emphasises that, under such circumstances, the analytic process

> must not be hurried by interpretations, however correct, since they may be felt as undue interference, as an attempt at devaluing the justification of their complaint and thus, instead of speeding up, they will slow down the therapeutic processes. (1968, p. 182)

However, sooner or later the time arrives when the analyst is compelled to address the patient's defensive pattern of repeating a familiar story and the sadomasochistic enactment inherent in such discourse. Failing to engage the patient in this interpretive undertaking, the analyst must be prepared to limit and even rupture the patient's manner of relating. Now the analyst explicitly refuses to listen to surface material and insists upon going deeper. This tactic is neither conventional nor risk-free. It can traumatise the patient and require much "damage control" sort of work. However, an intervention of this kind can also constitute the turning point in the analytic process and provide access to deeper configurations in the transference-countertransference axis.

Clinical vignette 35

> Rachel Rosenblatt is a school teacher in her mid-fifties. She has sought analysis with a vague fear of being purposeless, a lack of ability to commit herself to any pursuit in a meaningful way, and a sense that her marriage is emotionally over. She is vivacious and talkative. Her track record reveals her self-improvement from a lower middle class and rather provincial family background. She wants to grow, travel, and experience life in broader and deeper ways.
>
> A major and recurrent theme in her analysis is constituted by her attempts to "prove" to me that her husband Fred is intellectually dull and boring. Rachel recounts episode after episode, offers big and little details, to drive this point home. He does not respond to her appeals for "real" conversation, fails to say more than a word

or two after they walk out of a movie theatre, and responds in monosyllables when she recounts her day at the school where she teaches. She finds him very boring. He is driving her up the wall. Weeks pass and months turn into years but Rachel keeps bringing up more and more evidence of how boring Fred is.

My attempts to point out her insistent need to convince me and her implicit disbelief in my essential agreement with her go nowhere. When I link the "boring husband" scene with the unengaged mother of her childhood, she sees it but the material remains superficial. I feel helpless, annoyed, and, frankly, "bored"!

What is going on?, I ask myself and her. This is to little avail. Each day, Rachel has a fresh story with the same end: her husband was totally inept in conversation and was very boring. Time passes.

One day, she begins the session with "You know how Fred behaved last evening?" Sensing that the Tale of the Boring Husband is about to unfold for the four hundredth time, I respond by saying, "I am afraid that I am not interested in listening to last evening's details. But I am very interested in listening to your thoughts about why you want to tell me the same story over and over again. What do you get out of it? What do you think you are doing to me by such repetitions?" Rachel brushes me aside and proceeds to tell me about how boring her husband was the last evening. I interrupt and say, "No, I do not wish to hear the details of what happened last evening since I know that these would contain nothing new. What I *am* interested in is the need you feel to tell it to me as if I have not heard this story before and as if I do not agree with you." Rachel presses on. I challenge her again, noting silently to myself at this point that the sadomasochistic banter is slowly becoming a bit "delicious". Further speculations begin to arise in my mind, as a result.[2]

In essence, my RTL worked as a preparation for making an interpretation; it helped unmask a multilevelled transference relatedness that the patient was desperately seeking. While not putting it explicitly into words, by talking incessantly, the patient was trying to force me into the roles of (i) the "bored" part of herself with her playing the role of the boring husband (talking excessively being a great disguise for his monosyllabic speech), (ii) her disinterested mother whose attention she sorely wanted to engage as a child, and (iii) an uninvolved husband whom she nonetheless wanted to tell all her trivial and not-so-trivial experiences. There was much displacement and projective identification in operation here. Underneath it all was a longing for a mindless "container" (Bion, 1962b) who would absorb all her mental goings-on patiently and forever; this is projective identification turned malignant. The point, though, is that it was RTL that paved the way to the analysis of such hidden transferences.

RTL for "spoiling" the pleasure of excessive instinctual discharge

Another indication for refusing to listen is when the patient seems to be obtaining too much instinctual gratification by talking. That speech can become instinctualised has been noted from the earliest days of psychoanalysis. As mentioned above, Breuer and Freud (1895d) and Freud (1900a) recognised the sensory and magical quality of words and Ferenczi (1911) underscored the greater emotional power of obscenities in one's mother tongue as compared to those in a later-acquired language. Abraham observed that

> … we meet certain traits of character in people which can be traced back to a peculiar displacement within the oral sphere Their longing to experience gratification by way of sucking has changed to a need to *give* by way of the mouth, so that we find in them, besides the permanent longing to obtain everything, a constant need to communicate themselves orally to other people. This results in an obstinate urge to talk, connected in most cases with a feeling of overflowing. (1924, p. 401)

Later analysts (Fliess, 1949; Sharpe, 1940) have noted the contributions of anal and urethral discharge functions in patterns of speech. In addition, Loewenstein (1956) stated that a patient's way of talking may reveal that at times he uses speech for either seduction or aggression towards the analyst. A case in point is constituted by those borderline patients who frequently get enraged and scream loudly at their analysts. Getting emotionally flooded at the slightest misattunement on the therapist's part, they embark upon yelling, shouting obscenities, and at times, emitting blood-curdling screams. The first manifestation of such emotional flooding is usually a rapid

... accumulation of memories and fantasies that support the same emotion. The patient can refer to these memories or fantasies only in a kind of "shorthand"—fragmentary sentences, or a single word. He may then begin stuttering and lose the power of intelligible speech altogether. The patient may scream and exhibit diffuse motor activity; he may seem to have lost his human identity. (Volkan, 1976, p. 179)

Under such circumstances, the analyst ought to stay still, lay affectively low, say little except naming the affect (Katan, 1961) and, sometimes, address the patient by his or her first name (Volkan, 1976). Naming the emotion provides a cognitive handle for ego dominance and naming the person restores human identity, precluding the diabolical transformation caused by intense rage. These technical measures work well when screaming is occasional and transient. However, when such rage attacks are a matter of everyday occurrence and especially when the patient seems to be drawing great sadistic gratification from them, behavioural limits must be set. Kernberg's (1975, 1984; Kernberg, Selzer, Koenigsberg, Carr & Appelbaum, 1989, 2008) extensive writings on the treatment of borderline patients discuss such limit-setting in detail. Here it will suffice to say the analyst might refuse to listen to such screaming, firmly explaining to the patient that such behaviour adds little to the treatment process; in fact, it detracts from deepening their understanding of what is troubling to the patient at his or her core. Such acting out needs to be "controlled"[3] before it can become amenable to interpretation. In doing so, a partial and transient enactment of countertransference aggression might be inevitable.

Even the less overtly explosive forms of coercive talking on the patient's part can evoke powerful reactions from the therapist. The following recollection by a respected colleague attests to this.

Clinical vignette 36

I looked at my watch and realized it was time for my regular Wednesday session with Annabelle Wright. Perhaps she would cancel. She often did, though usually she gave me more notice than this. I found myself hoping she would be late. That was possible. In fact, it was probable. The thought energized me enough to open my door gently. But there she was, filling her cup with water, looking up and catching my eye. My heart sank.

Annabelle was a thirty-four-year-old struggling actress who had experienced significant trauma as a child. With two substance abusing parents, she had been lucky to have made it out of her home environment alive. And that was no exaggeration since violence was not infrequent in her childhood home. For any other patient, I would have felt the utmost sympathy. Her story was supposedly compelling, her strength and fortitude admirable. However, somehow, all I felt was cloudy. When Annabelle talked, I lost focus. Try as I might, I could not grab onto anything meaningful. She spoke in vagaries, talking intensely and rapidly, but really saying nothing of meaning. She used psychologically astute language that was seemingly insightful, yet upon examination, lacked the depth I at first attributed to her words. And she often spoke for the entire length of a session, giving me little opportunity to intervene. At times, towards the session's end, I would try to say something but she thwarted that effort and continued talking. Over and over again I failed to get her to leave my office until five minutes after the session was supposed to have ended.

I could have handled Annabelle's barrage of words if it had not been for the hostility that emanated from her pores. She arrived shooting darts in my direction with her looks, and glaring at me, waiting for me to somehow offend. I often thought to myself that if looks could kill, I would be dead.

Inevitably, I would utter something that to others would have been benign, but to Annabelle was mortally wounding. My asking about her partner meant I had not listened to her in the session before. My suggesting she felt unresolved about her past meant I lacked empathy for her current situation. My attempts at empathizing meant I could not give her the insight she needed in order to better her predicament. She came to session with a goal in mind and if I so much as dared to interrupt or shift course, she told me in no uncertain terms that she did not feel it would be helpful to go in that direction. She would then continue to tell me what she felt "we" should be exploring though without making me a partner to the conversation. I felt held hostage. The stream of her words felt like a rope that was tightening around me and suffocating me. And so, that day, as Annabelle talked on, my eyes felt heavy.

I felt overwhelmingly tired, exhausted. And I felt slightly panicky, anxious that she was going to "test" me on my listening skills and that I was going to be found wanting. The haze descended though, against my will, and I eventually succumbed. (Helen Engal, personal communication, January 2011)

The presence of hostility in incessant talking is a matter approached by Aulagnier from a novel perspective.

If one considers the auditory function, what one notes is the absence in this register of any system of closure comparable to the closing of eyelids or lips, or to the tactile retreat that muscular movement allows. The auditory cavity can not remove itself from the irruption of sound waves; it is an open orifice in which, in a state of waking, the outside continuously penetrates … [consequently] the voice-object may so easily become the embodiment of the persecutory object. (2001, p. 60)

Aulagnier adds that since the quality of (mother's) voice can enhance or rupture any pleasure that her child is experiencing, the patient's experience of the analyst's tone is extremely important. And, one might add, so is the quality of the patient's voice. The snippet of countertransference experience above amply testifies to this. The acid of hatred dripped from every word the patient spoke.

In contrast is the marked libidinal gratification extracted from talking by some patients. Here too, the communicative function of speech is eclipsed. One category of such patients is formed by sexual perverts and the other by narcissists. The pervert can resort to talking in a highly sexualised manner, lingering just a bit longer on sexual details, and uttering the name of genitals with ever-so-slightly wet emphasis. At other times, he does not resort to "dirty talk" and yet seems to be having sex via talking. The narcissist can also utilise speaking for purposes other than communication. Bach notes that

"… in the narcissistic state, language is used predominantly in an autocentric manner to regulate well-being or self-esteem, rather than in an allocentric manner for purposes of communicating with or understanding an object. Thus the emphasis is less on the communicative function and more on the genetically earlier manipulative function of words, which may be used to frighten or to soothe, to distance or to merge, to control or to be controlled .... Because language is used more manipulatively or as a substitute for more primitive, proximal and autocentric modalities, such as touch, taste, and smell, one has the overall sense that the language is impoverished, although at times, it may be rhetorically brilliant. (1977, pp. 218–219)

The analyst must attempt to unmask such perverse and narcissistic uses of language. Confronting the patient—at first, gently, but, if the pattern persists, firmly—with his hidden agenda might draw a wedge between what the patient says and how he says it. This, in turn, can be used for deepening the awareness of the transference that is operative when such speaking is deployed. However, this is easier said than done. Instinctualised speech patterns of such sorts are deeply embedded in character; they are ego-syntonic and pleasurable. Therefore, it might become necessary to "block" them in their earliest and nascent state by calling attention to the essentially hostile (in the case of paranoid patients), juicy (in the case of the pervert), and self-soothing (in the case of the narcissist) quality of speech and letting the patient know that one would refuse to listen any further if the patient talks in this manner. Paradoxically, it is such a blockage that often brings out into consciousness the particular self-object relationship that was being played out by "swearing", "dirty talk", or "narcissistic rambling".[4]

RTL for playful and ironical purposes during the termination phase

Finally, there is the fourth indication for refusing to listen and this is when a thoroughly analysed transference resurfaces a day or two before the mutually agreed-upon date of termination. There is often an ironic, if not humorous, tenor to such an occurrence. This is evident in the following vignette lent to me by a distinguished colleague.

Clinical vignette 37

David Conn, a thirty-six-year-old man, grew up with a sense that his father did not like him. He yearned for paternal love and in the course of his analysis oscillated between defending against imagined criticism from me and desperately seeking my approval and praise. Years of interpreting the implicit Oedipal transference and painstakingly deconstructing the projective distortion of his father's image led to a real-life rapprochement between him and his father. Within the analysis, too, tension lessened. His hostile competitive impulses could now come to the surface and undergo genetic linking as well as ego-modulation toward healthy work-related ambition. A termination date was mutually agreed upon in the sixth year of his treatment. Matters proceeded more or less according to expectation. Then, in the very last session, David said, "You know, I find myself wondering all over again if you do secretly hate me. What if ..." I interrupted him with an exaggerated and clearly mock groan, saying, "No, no. Please don't tell me this now. I don't want to hear this now!" David burst out laughing and the session moved toward its last minutes with us saying goodbye to each other from a position of mutual regard and affection. (Vamik Volkan, personal communication, February 11, 2011)

Here the analyst's refusal to listen had an entirely different purpose than it did in the other vignettes cited above. Done at a stage in treatment when the existence of respectful mutuality within the dyad was taken for granted and when there was little time left for interpretation, the RTL intended to remind the patient that he now had some choice in surrendering to regression or not. That the analyst emitted a mock groan while declaring his RTL and that the patient responded to it by laughing confirms that the spirit of playfulness behind the intervention was known to both.

Concluding remarks

In this chapter I have noted that, at times, speech itself can serve as a resistance to the analytic process. I have then raised the tricky question of whether listening is always "good" and helpful. I have suggested that the analyst might actually refuse to listen: (i) when the patient is attempting to pull the analyst into a misalliance from the very beginning of their contact, (ii) when the patient is repeating something *ad nauseam*, (iii) when the patient is using speech predominantly for instinctual discharge or narcissistic stabilisation, and (iv) when the patient is bringing forth a much-analysed transference in an unconsciously playful manner towards the end of the analysis.[5] I have emphasised that in general, RTL is a technical strategy that (i) should be utilised only by those with considerable experience in conducting analyses along the customary lines, (ii) should be used sparingly and only when one or the other of the indications delineated above is clearly present, (iii) should be used after much listening, affirmative interventions, and interpretive work has been done, (iv) is reserved for later phases of long analyses, (v) should be made after consultation with a colleague and, if that is not possible, its use must be discussed post hoc with a colleague, (vi) should be used after an earnest effort has been made to disentangle countertransference temptations from genuine therapeutic intent, and (vii) requires that its impact upon the patient be looked for and analytically handled.

Also to be underscored is that even when the analyst uses RTL, the analyst actually does not stop listening. What he does stop is listening to the surface material. The analyst, who has heard five hundred times about a parent's indifference to the patient, might raise his hand and say, "You know what, I am not really interested in listening to this tale all over again but I am very interested in why you feel driven to tell it to me again and again as if I never heard it." Seeming to not listen (to surface material), the analyst actually shows that he is more attuned (i.e., "listening") to what might be lurking behind the patient's need to repeat something endlessly. In effect, such "refusing to listen" constitutes an "interpretive action" (Ogden, 1994; see also Chapter Six in this book). It is the analyst's way of saying that "Look, let us not get derailed by derivative phenomena and/or get caught up in an instinctual enactment. Instead, let us focus upon the need you have for such manoeuvres and upon the anxieties that propel this need."

The theoretical rationale for the intervention I have outlined here rests upon the fact that listening, like all other human functions, can become detached from ego control and come to lie under the domination of the id or superego. In other words, the function of listening itself can become instinctualised[6]. One might go on listening to endless repetitions or instinctualised discourse as a form of masochistic submission to the patient. One might also keep on listening eternally because one has come to idealise listening; the more one listens the better one is in the eyes of internalised analytic ideals. This complication can doom the analyst and render his listening to be ultimately superego driven. Needless to stay that this problem is more likely to occur among candidates and those striving to become training analysts, since both these groups remain dependent upon third party approval of technique.

To my mind, the patient's violent screaming and "dirty talk" has to be forcefully stopped, if gentler efforts at confrontation and interpretation do not seem to be going anywhere. I also believe that endless listening to repetitive material is a perversion of the analytic attitude. This too should not be allowed to develop or continue for long. The pathological optimism underlying the patient's repetition needs to be confronted and, in tenacious cases, ruptured. Basically, it comes down to "having to state that neither analysis nor analyst is an omnipotent rescuer, as the patients in their illusion needed to believe" (Amati-Mehler & Argentieri, 1989, p. 301). The intervention is intended to inject "optimal disillusionment" (Gedo & Goldberg, 1973) in the clinical interaction and demands that the analysand learn to give up magical thinking. The self-object related fantasies as well as the unconscious instinctual pleasure associated with monotonous repetitions, screaming fits, and sexualised conversation can only then come to the surface. Putting an end to all this might be a bit traumatic to the patient but it might also constitute a turning point of the analytic process provided, of course, the analyst's holding functions are in place and the effect of such a confrontational intervention can be analysed.

All in all, listening is good. Listening patiently for a long time is better. But listening forever to material that is all too familiar or highly instinctualised constitutes a collusion with the patient's sadomasochism and narcissism. Such listening is contrary to the purposes of psychoanalysis.

Notes

1. I had mentioned this intervention earlier (Akhtar, 2009, 2011b) but with less clinical detail and theoretical elucidation.
2. The point here is not *what* those speculations were but that the blocking of her "manic" talk allowed them to occur.
3. Freud's recommendation of giving a "sharp reprimand" (1917, p. 248) to patients who leave the door open as they enter the analyst's office is essentially in the same spirit. The aim of what he recommended and what I am suggesting here is the same, which is to "force" a behavioural discharge back into the realm of thinking and conversation.

4. Such instinctual discharge with talking must be distinguished from "affectualization" (Bibring, Dwyer, Huntington & Valenstein, 1961), which denotes a characterological tendency to overemphasise the emotional aspects of an issue in order to avoid a deeper, rational aspect of understanding. This type of habitual deployment of "emotionality as a defense" (Siegman, 1954) is more diffuse than the specific instinctual discharge via speaking.

5. Not included among these indications are situations where "refusing to listen" occurs as a part of the analyst's aborting a session altogether. The latter might become necessary if the analyst feels physically very ill during the session or if it is discovered that the patient (e.g., a single mother) has left a young child unattended at home in order to come for her analysis.

6. Among aspects of psychoanalytic enterprise, the couch is similarly vulnerable to idealisation, giving rise to the belief that no psychoanalytic work can be done unless the patient is in a recumbent posture.

CHAPTER SEVEN

Listening in non-clinical situations

"For as soon as anyone deliberately concentrates his attention to a certain degree, he begins to select from the material before him; one point will be fixed in his mind with particular clearness and some other will be correspondingly disregarded"

—Sigmund Freud (1912e, p. 112)

L ike a cardiologist's stethoscope or a surgeon's scalpel, psycho-analytic listening is our prime ally and instrument. We use it, depend upon it, and seek to sharpen it all the time. However, the respect we accord it must go further; it should involve measures to protect the sanctity of this important function. One measure to safe-guard the functional astuteness and moral integrity of psychoanalytic listening paradoxically comes from limiting its use. While this state-ment might appear curious, more strange is the fact that textbooks of psychoanalysis (Moore & Fine, 1995; Nersessian & Kopf, 1996; Person, Cooper & Gabbard, 2005) and monographs on psychoanalytic tech-nique (Etchegoyen, 1999; Fenichel, 1941; Greenson, 1967; Volkan, 2010) make no mention of the limits and bounds of analytic listening. This might be due to their focusing exclusively on the clinical encounter and not upon the analyst's listening, thinking, and speaking functions in non-clinical situations. The latter are left unaddressed and it is taken for granted that the psychoanalyst would know when to use his analytic mind and when to put it aside. However, many analysts continue to listen and talk in an analytic manner outside the clinical situation. They even take pride in being an analyst "all the time".

I have reservations about such an attitude. Analytic listening, to my mind, begins to lose it edge and its usefulness the farther one carries it from the clinical set-up; the only exception to this is the analyst's self-analysis which continues beyond his working hours anyway (see Sonnenberg, 1995, especially in this regard). Indeed, in this chapter, I propose—and discuss in some depth—three situations where an analyst must (i) limit the scope of analytic listening, (ii) temper the use of analytic listening, and (iii) put analytic listening aside altogether. The analyst's conduct during supervision of candidates,[1] his or her attention to the discourse in public media, and his or her receptiveness to ordinary conversations at home constitute these three situations, respectively.

Analytic supervision

In supervising the analytic treatment of "control" cases by candidates in training, the psychoanalyst takes on two roles. First, he functions as a teacher and imparts knowledge of the craft, the component skills, and the theory of psychoanalytic technique. Second, he functions as a psychoanalyst and listens to the material being presented to him in a psychoanalytic manner. Haesler (1993) has lucidly described these two roles and, more importantly, the tripartite focus of the supervisor's psychoanalytic attention. The latter consists of psychoanalytically listening to (i) the conscious, preconscious, and unconscious dynamics of the candidate's patient and how he or she relates to the candidate, (ii) the dynamic processes occurring within the clinical dyad, and (iii) the candidate's "ways of responding both to the patient's material and to what he is hearing from, and experiencing with, the supervisor" (p. 550). Haesler emphasises that discerning and pointing out the blind spots in the candidate's relationship to the clinical material at hand is a crucial task of the supervisor and that he can recognise such scotoma only by listening analytically to the candidate's presentation.

The supervisor's addressing such countertransference difficulties on the candidate's part, however, does not mean that he should get involved in analysing the latter's personal conflicts. Any temptation to do so must be avoided and the focus of analytic listening must be narrowed down to the candidate's relationship to the patient, the patient's material, and the supervisory process. His or her blind spots (e.g., consistent inability to follow up on the patient's saying that he visits "gentlemen's clubs", invariably changing the topic when it comes to racial matters) should be looked upon as emotional responses to the clinical process and not traced to the candidate's internal objects, private fantasies, and childhood experiences.

> Thus, if a candidate tends to be rather hesitant, for instance, in taking up a specific dynamic issue within the treatment of his patient due to a countertransference response, this hesitancy should *not* be reflected and dealt with, within the supervisory situation, as a specific neurotic or personality trait of the candidate, but rather as a specific response to the patient, or resonance phenomenon within the candidate, and the specific dynamic interaction between himself and the patient. Only by attempting to clarify any relational activities strictly from this point of view will it, eventually, become possible to differentiate and to clarify, together with the candidate, any influence not resulting from the process but from the personality of the candidate. Such a differentiation and clarification may then eventually lead to a mutual understanding that there is something within the supervisory relation that may best be dealt with not in the supervision, but in the personal analysis of the candidate. (Ibid., p. 551, italics added)

In all fairness, though, it should be noted that Haesler's position reflects one pole of the ongoing controversy regarding the desirability of an overlap between analytic supervision and the candidate's personal analysis. Haesler seeks to restrict this overlap. Others think differently. Grotjahn (1955), for instance, advocated that the supervisor actively interpret the candidate's countertransference on the basis of the candidate-patient interaction and the candidate-supervisor relationship. This proposal found support in the notion of a "parallel process" existing between the analytic and the supervisory situations (Hora, 1957; Searles, 1955), whereby the candidate is viewed as re-enacting the dissociated aspects of his clinical experience in the supervisory situation. Fleming and Benedek (1966), too, saw analytic supervision as an opportunity for the analysis of the candidate's countertransference to his patient.

In contrast, Arlow (1963) emphasised that "It would be erroneous to conclude that the main function of the supervisor is to consider the therapist's countertransference and to deal with it during supervision in an analytic way" (p. 582). Levenson (1982) went a step further and declared that such a "meta-therapeutic" style of supervision can become extremely uncomfortable for the candidate, especially when placed in the hands of a sadistic supervisor. Rilton (1988) also stated that "The supervisor cannot and should not try to interpret the candidate's personal problems and conflicts" (p. 113). Indeed, there are analysts (e.g., Levy, 1995) who strenuously refrain from interpreting countertransference difficulties and from pointing out the so-called "parallel process" phenomena.

In a lucid and comprehensive discussion of such divergences, Pegeron (1996) acknowledged that the candidate's "countertransference difficulties cannot be resolved in supervision. However, supervision can be an effective stimulus for self-analysis and continued work on one's own analysis" (p. 700). For him, the candidate's

> learning problems are based on conflict and resistance, [and] conflict and resistance occur in both supervisee and supervisor and require active dynamic immediacy in order to be effectively addressed. This sets in motion the working-through process necessary to facilitate learning and the development of one's analytic identity ... This approach to supervision, while mindful of its limitations— i.e., that it is not treatment but rather a way of developing the candidate's analytic self—provides a different but more "analytic" experience. By "analytic experience" I mean an experience that facilitates analysis, that permits the candidate to understand features of his own analysis more concretely. (Ibid., pp. 698–700).

What becomes clear from this quick survey of the literature on analytic supervision is that: (i) the supervisor *does* listen like an analyst during the supervisory hours, (ii) such listening yields important data about the candidate's analytic work ego, besides of course the analytic process between him and the patient, (iii) while listening analytically might give rise to speculations about the candidate's character, the supervisor realises that he or she lacks corroborative data, does not have consent from the candidate to comment upon his character, and he is not the candidate's analyst, and (iv) while he can (and should) point out the candidate's blind spots and countertransference resistances, his "interpretive" remarks are better limited to the impact of these difficulties upon the process of treatment and supervision; for further understanding of the candidate's difficulties, the supervisor encourages him to bring out what they have touched upon in his personal analysis. All in all, therefore, there is some diminution of the expanse of the supervisor's analytic listening along with a comparable restraint upon his interpretive activity. Solnit's (1970) comment that "Supervision is more than teaching and less than treatment" (p. 360) perhaps says it all.

Public discourse

A second situation affecting the analyst's habitual use of analytic listening involves his encounter with public discourse. Parapraxes, lapses of memory, gross mispronunciations, awkward pauses, and clever "sliding of meanings" (Horowitz, 1975) during cocktail parties, political speeches, news reports, or celebrity interviews tug at the psychoanalyst's auditory sleeve, imploring him to give them his customary clinical attention. Such temptation must be warded off despite the narcissistic pleasure it promises to provide. The following incident demonstrates this point.

On the morning of November 10, 2011, a reporter from *The Philadelphia Inquirer*, the leading local newspaper, called me. He wanted my opinion about the gaffe made by Texas Governor Rick Perry during the previous night's Republican Primary contestants' debate. I had watched the debate on television and knew what the reporter was talking about. Perry, while enthusiastically declaring his plans to reduce the size of federal government—were he to be elected president—had made a shocking parapraxis. Here are his words:

> Let me tell you, there's three agencies of government that are gone when I get there," Perry said. "Commerce, education and the, um, uh, what's the third one there … commerce, education and the, um, EPA?" When asked by Scott Pelley, the moderator, if he could name the third agency of government, Perry answered "the third agency

of government, I would do away with: education, commerce and let's see … the third one, I can't. Oops. (thedailybeast.com/2011/articles)

The newspaper reporter asked me what I made of Perry's forgetting the name of the third agency he would eliminate as president. In other words, how did I listen to it as a psychoanalyst? Now this was a significant moment. It stirred up mixed feelings in me. On the one hand, I was impressed by this reporter's interest in seeking the opinion of a psychoanalyst; this conveyed his respect for the complexities of the human mind. On the other hand, could I, in all honesty, give a genuinely psychoanalytic opinion on this matter? Was I listening as a psychoanalyst to the Republican primary debate or merely as a politically interested citizen?

Let me put such inner meanderings aside and tell you what I did say to the reporter. In essence, I told him that I had never met Governor Perry and did not know him as a person at all. I did not know his parents, his early teachers, and other important figures of his formative years. I also did not know his wife and children. In other words, I had no familiarity with the world of his internal objects and therefore could not say anything that would *specifically* apply to the governor and to his forgetting. However, I could make a general remark regarding such curious moments of amnesia and that would include variables of an overwhelmingly busy schedule, physical fatigue, aging brain, and perhaps, some guilty self-punishment; after all, by the time he had named the two Departments of Commerce and Education, he had, in effect, laid off hundreds of people from their jobs. And, the subsequent pang of guilt, perhaps, made him forget the third department.

Now, this sounded all fine and dandy. However, as I gave it more thought afterwards, other possibilities surfaced in my mind. Could it be that the governor had a friend or relative in the department he forgot? After all, who wants to lay off a loved one from his or her job? Could it be that someone from that department had once done a big favour for the governor and therefore, closing that department forever would reflect utter ingratitude (besides causing remorse)? And, so on and so forth.

The point I am trying to make is this: one could not have correctly deduced the meaning of Governor Perry's lapse of memory without knowing a lot more about him as a person and about his "relationship" to the department whose name he forgot. One simply would not know what the parapraxis meant. To be sure, we psychoanalysts get tempted to over-extend the reach of our psychoanalytic listening (and the conclusions drawn from it) to include snippets of public conversations. A slip of the tongue made by someone in a cocktail party, a dinner guest's calling the host by someone else's name, and a politician making a blustering gaffe (e.g., Mitt Romney's declaration that he has been married to "the same woman for twenty-five—oops, forty-two—years," in the same Republican debate) readily perk up our analytic ears but we must restrain ourselves. The analytic greed stirred up by such tempting morsels of unconscious activity must be controlled. We must remind ourselves that we lack data—developmental history, associations, currently active psychodynamic conflicts, dreams, transferences, etc.—to listen in a true analytic manner to such material.[2] The allure of becoming omniscient oracles must be renounced at such moments.

Life at home

Having considered the restrictions on analytic listening during supervision and the need to hesitate before applying analytic listening to public discourse, we can move on to a situation that requires a psychoanalyst to put his analytic listening aside altogether. This involves the analyst's domestic life. Allow me to illustrate my point by presenting two imaginary (but plausible) scenes to you.

Scene one: The analyst is waiting for his first patient of the day. The patient, a junior doctor in a nearby hospital, arrives in time, rushed and breathless. Lying on the couch, he catches his breath and begins talking. Here is what he says:

> The morning was awful. After getting ready for the day, I came downstairs … went into the kitchen. I wanted to drink some orange juice. So, I opened the fridge door … I swear by God I wish I had not. Something in the fridge smelled so badly that I gagged. In fact, I almost threw up. I don't know if the milk I'd bought a few days ago had spoiled, or there was something wrong with the fridge itself. The stink was terrible, I tell you.

The analyst listens to his patient and senses his distress, can almost experience the awful smell and the subsequent gagging response himself.

He feels bad for his patient. Gradually, however, his reverie spreads to the unlit periphery of what he has just heard. He wonders what it is that the patient actually is talking about in the guise of this "rotten milk—broken fridge" scenario? Does the patient want sympathy? Is he asking to be given something to drink by the analyst? Could this disguise a deeper wish to be breastfed? Is there a fellatio fantasy lurking somewhere here? Or, might the patient's report contain a dim recall of a maternal breast abscess during his infancy? As such possibilities begin to populate the analyst's mind, it becomes clear that—unbeknown to himself—he has put his "ordinary" listening aside. He is certainly *not* thinking about refrigerator repair, money, warranties, and so on.

Scene two: The analyst arrives at his office to find a message on his answering machine that his first patient of the day has cancelled the appointment. Finding himself unexpectedly free, the analyst goes to his computer and begins to check his email. The phone rings. It is his wife. Here is what she says:

> The morning was awful. After getting ready for the day, I came downstairs ... went into the kitchen. I wanted to drink some orange juice. So, I opened the fridge door ... I swear by God I wish I had not. Something in the fridge smelled so badly that I gagged. In fact, I almost threw up. I don't know if the milk I'd bought a few days ago had spoiled, or there was something wrong with the fridge itself. The stink was terrible, I tell you.

The analyst listens to his wife and senses her distress, can almost experience the awful smell and the subsequent gagging response himself. He feels bad for her. Soon, the thought occurs to him: what if the fridge is really broken? He tries to recall how old the fridge actually is. He also finds himself wondering about the electric connections and circuit breakers in their house that might have led to the trouble. He desperately searches his mind about whether the fridge is still under warranty. If not, how much is the repair going to cost? Or, would they have to buy a new one? As such possibilities begin to populate the analyst's mind, it becomes clear that—unbeknown to himself—he has put his "analytic" listening aside. He is certainly *not* thinking about breastfeeding, fellatio fantasies, maternal breast abscess, and so on.

The juxtaposition of these admittedly synthetic scenarios is intended to underscore the fact that *not listening* in an analytic manner is as crucial at home as listening analytically is during one's clinical work. And, by implication, a related message is that listening analytically to one's family members can be as disastrous as not listening analytically to one's patients. Since I have already addressed the latter at some length (see Chapter Five), I will say a few things here about the former, that is, the problem posed by listening analytically to one's spouse, children, siblings, etc. Doing so seems wrong for four reasons:

- We do not have their *consent* for our listening to them in an analytic manner.
- We do not have adequate *data* about what they are actually thinking, feeling, and perceiving at any given moment. We do not know what they dreamt the night before our conversation. We cannot ask them to free-associate. We hear only what they tell us in a consciously tailored and socially censored fashion.
- We do not have a *purpose* in listening psychoanalytically to our family members; we are not "treating" them and our "analytic" observations are unlikely to "cure" them. We can be loving, empathic, and helpful without being their therapists.
- We hardly follow clinical *ethics* if we insist upon listening analytically without consent, adequate data, and therapeutic purpose.

In light of this, it is unlikely to come as a surprise that family members resent being treated as analytic patients. Though my experience is modest and limited to only two cases (which, due to reasons of confidentiality, I cannot describe in detail), I am convinced that the recipients of such "domestic analysis" invariably feel misunderstood and violated. This is especially so since the supposedly hidden aspects revealed by the wise spouse/parent analyst are almost always negative ("Darling, you are using a lot of projection here", "I wonder if you can see the hidden aggression in your comment", "You appear awfully regressed and infantile", and so on). The supposed "patient" is shown his weakness and character defects, never his covert strengths and goodness. That sadism has put on a mask of psychoanalysis here goes without saying.

In commenting upon therapists' tendency to treat their children as analysands, Maeder notes that:

> The use of therapeutic concepts and techniques may become habitual and excessive, and rather than enhancing one's ability to act

as a responsible and loving parent, may come to replace it, and not solely when there are problematic situations, but all the time. Parents can live by the book and neglect those spontaneous emotional responses that, although sometimes damaging, are also the foundation of parent-child relations. Quasi-therapeutic interventions may be intentional or may be reflexive carryovers from a life in the office that has not been fully left behind at the end of the day. (1989, p. 121)

Maeder goes on to illustrate the ludicrous, if not harmful, effects of carrying the psychoanalytic attitude into one's relationship with one's children by providing the following vignette.

Martin Deutsch remembers his annoyance when he was around six years old and painted a picture of a soldier. The soldier, naturally enough at the time, was wearing a sword at his side, and his mother, analyst Helene Deutsch, promptly insisted that it was a penis. No, he said, it was a sword. "She insisted that it was a penis—this sort of thing happened all the time—and after a while I gave up. Obviously I was supposed to absorb this analytic concept, that when something hangs somewhere, one is supposed to say that it's a penis. Now I know that in some sense this is true, but why do you have to tell a kid that? What did it really have to do with me and my drawing? (Ibid., p. 137)

What needs to be understood here is that there are two risks in the analyst-parent (or spouse) making an "interpretation" of such a sort.[3] The first involves the conjecture being completely off the mark, a possibility not too far-fetched given the fact that one often has little corroborative data in such circumstances. The second risk is that one's interpretation is right. This is even more traumatising since to abruptly reveal something unconscious or disguised to someone overlooks the subject's need to remain unaware of that aspect.[4] Feldman has emphasised this point in a paper on addressing disavowed self-representations in the clinical situation.

If the patient has needed to split-off and project unacceptable parts of the self, the analyst has to consider how useful it is to describe the situation to the patient who may no longer be in contact with the disavowed parts. The disadvantage of the situation is that an interpretation that refers to different parts of the personality may make sense intellectually, but may in fact reinforce the patient's defensive structure. (2007, p. 371)

The degree of hurt caused by such ill-advised interventions is multi-plied many fold in the context of familial relationships. A comment like "Sweetheart, don't you see the hidden grandiosity behind your giving our children this gift?" can be experienced as an ice-pick driven into the breast of generosity. It is therefore best to avoid listening and talking in analytic ways at home. One is often incorrect, frequently hurtful, and always unethical in doing so.

This applies to situations where only one family member is a psycho-analyst. What happens when two or more are psychoanalysts? A common situation is two analysts married to each other. Do the ideas I have outlined above apply to them also? I think so. However, an occasional playful exchange using analytic jargon between them might be una-voidable. Even then, a "pretend mode" (Target & Fonagy, 1996)[5] must be maintained and the dialogue should avoid assaults on each other's character. Love and mutual respect within the couple helps prevent such derailment. If hostility prevails in the relationship, analytic "inter-pretations" of each other's behaviour can readily camouflage destruc-tive intent.

Concluding remarks

In this last chapter of my book on analytic listening, I have attempted to demonstrate the restrictions we must put on this prized capacity of ours. Just as we would not drive a Rolls-Royce in a muddy field or wear a dinner jacket at a garden barbecue, we must not overextend and misapply psychoanalytic listening to all sorts of things we hear. In supervision, we should restrict our analytic listening to the control patient's material and to the patient-candidate relationship, eliminating speculation about the candidate's internal object and his or her overall character. In public discourse, we must temper the risk of becoming a "wild analyst" and remind ourselves of the inappropriateness of the setting and the lack of supportive data. In domestic life, we should try to put analytic listening aside as much as possible and not let techni-cal jargon crowd out the vernacular of "ordinary" human conversation.

Such restraints on the use of our analytic minds paradoxically sharpen their edge. Remember, a surgeon would not use his scalpel for pruning shrubs in his garden nor would a cardiologist his stethoscope to hear songs from a CD player. Everything has its time and place and psychoanalytic listening is no exception to this rule.

Notes

1. Since this chapter is titled "Listening in non-clinical situations", it seems only fair to acknowledge that supervision of control cases is not entirely a "non-clinical" enterprise.
2. In effect, such caution should extend to almost all ventures in "applied psychoanalysis".
3. The well-known psychoanalyst, Ira Brenner, thinks that constant childhood exposure to psychoanalytic terminology while being raised by analyst parents can compromise the future analysability of the offspring (personal communication, February 19, 2012).
4. I myself was considerably traumatised by someone who interviewed me while I was applying for analytic training; this person bluntly pointed out certain aspects of my character that were entirely out of my awareness at that time and caused me great distress.
5. Target and Fonagy's term for an operational feature of the young child's psyche which has the following characteristics: (1) knowledge that internal experience might not reflect the facts and events of external reality; (2) separation of internal and external realities with the accompanying assumption that an internal state has no impact upon external reality; and (3) selective incorporation of facets of external reality in the unfolding inner experience. The "pretend mode" of mental functioning is most clearly evident when the child is playing; he can readily entertain a belief useful for his play activity while in reality knowing it to be false. According to Target and Fonagy the "pretend mode" of functioning gives access to processes and knowledge which would not otherwise be consciously available … thus playing or pretending at times reveals surprising abilities, while at other times it offers opportunities for regression and the expression of unconscious cries (pp. 465-466).

REFERENCES

Abbasi, A. (2008). Who's side are you on?: Muslim analysts analyzing non-Muslim patients. In: S. Akhtar (Ed.), *The Crescent and the Couch: Cross Currents between Islam and Psychoanalysis* (pp. 335–350). New York: Other Press.

Abraham, K. (1924). The influence of oral eroticism on character formation. In: *Selected Papers of Karl Abraham, M. D.* (pp. 393–406). New York: Brunner/Mazel.

Abrams, D. M. (1991). Looking at and looking away: Etiology of preoedipal splitting in a deaf girl. *Psychoanalytic Study of the Child, 46*: 277–304.

Akhtar, S. (1992). Tethers, orbits, and invisible fences: clinical, developmental, sociocultural, and technical aspects of optimal distance. In: S. Kramer S. Akhtar (Eds.), *When the Body Speaks: Psychological Meanings in Kinetic Clues* (pp. 21–57). Northvale, NJ: Jason Aronson.

Akhtar, S. (1993). Review of *Being a Character: Psychoanalysis and Self Experience* by Christopher Bollas. *Psychoanalytic Books, 4*: 519–530.

Akhtar, S. (1996). "Someday ..." and "if only ..." fantasies: pathological optimism and inordinate nostalgia as related forms of idealization. *Journal of American Psychoanalytic Association, 44*: 723–753.

Akhtar, S. (1999). *Immigration and Identity: Turmoil, Treatment, and Transformation.* Northvale, NJ: Jason Aronson.

Akhtar, S. (2000). From schisms through synthesis to informed oscillation: An attempt at integrating some diverse aspects of psychoanalytic technique. *Psychoanalytic Quarterly, 69*: 265–288.

Akhtar, S. (2006). Technical challenges faced by the immigration analyst. *Psychoanalytic Quarterly, 75*: 21–43.

Akhtar, S. (Ed.) (2007). *Listening to Others: Developmental and Clinical Aspects of Empathy and Attunement.* Lanham, MD: Jason Aronson.

Akhtar, S. (2009). *Comprehensive Dictionary of Psychoanalysis.* London: Karnac.

Akhtar, S. (2011a). *Immigration and Acculturation: Mourning, Adaptation, and the Next Generation.* Lanham, MD: Jason Aronson.

Akhtar, S. (2011b). Refusing to listen to certain kinds of material. In: S. Akhtar (Ed.), *Unusual Interventions: Alterations of Frame, Method, and Relationship in Psychotherapy and Psychoanalysis* (pp. 83–98). London: Karnac.

Akhtar, S. & Buckman, J. (1977). Differential diagnosis of mutism: A review and a report of three unusual cases. *Diseases of the Nervous System, 38*: 558–563.

Akhtar, S. & Parens, H. (2001). *Does God Help?: Development and Clinical Aspects of Religious Belief.* Northvale, NJ: Jason Aronson.

Amati-Mehler, J. & Argentieri, S. (1989). Hope and hopelessness: A technical problem? *International Journal of Psychoanalysis, 70*: 295–304.

Amati-Mehler, J., Argentieri, S. & Canestri, J. (1993). *The Babel of the Unconscious: Mother Tongue and Foreign Languages in the Psychoanalytic Dimension.* J. Whitelaw-Cucco (Trans.). Madison, CT: International Universities Press.

Anthi, P. R. (1983). Reconstruction of preverbal experiences. *Journal of the American Psychoanalytic Association, 31*: 33–58.

Arlow, J. A. (1961). Silence and the theory of technique. *Journal of the American Psychoanalytic Association, 9*: 44–55.

Arlow, J. A. (1963). The supervisory situation. *Journal of the American Psychoanalytic Association, 11*: 576–594.

Arlow, J. A. (1995). Stilted listening: Psychoanalysis as discourse. *Psychoanalytic Quarterly, 64*: 215–233.

Aron, L. (1991). The patient's experience of the analyst's subjectivity. *Psychoanalytic Dialogues, 1*: 29–51.

Atwood, B. (2007). The Australian patient: traumatic pasts and the work of history. In: M. T. S. Hooke & S. Akhtar (Eds.), *The Geography of Meanings: Psychoanalytic Perspectives on Place, Space, Land, and Dislocation* (pp. 63–78). London: International Psychoanalytical Association.

Aulagnier, P. (1979). *Destinies of Pleasure.* Paris: Presses Universitaires de France.

Aulagnier, P. (2001). *The Violence of Interpretation: From Pictogram to Statement.* London: Brunner/Routledge.

Bach, S. (1977). On the narcissistic state of consciousness. *International Journal of Psychoanalysis, 58*: 209–233.

Bacon, R. (2000). Theory and therapeutics: Stress in the analytic identity. *Free Associations, 8*: 1–20.

Balint, M. (1968). *The Basic Fault: Therapeutic Aspects of Regression.* London: Tavistock.

Baranger, M. (2009). The mind of the analyst: from listening to interpretation. In: M. Baranger & W. Baranger (Eds.), *The Work of Confluence* (pp. 89–106). London: Karnac.

Baranger, M. & Baranger, W. (Eds.) (2009). *The Work of Confluence.* London: Karnac.

Benjamin, J. (1995). Recognition and destruction: An outline of intersubjectivity. In: *Like Subjects, Love Objects.* New Haven, CT: Yale University Press.

Benjamin, J. (2004). Beyond doer and done-to: An intersubjective view of thirdness. *Psychoanalytic Quarterly, 73*: 5–46.

Benjamin, J. (2007). Listening together: Intersubjective aspects of the analytic process of losing and restoring recognition. In: S. Akhtar (Ed.), *Listening To Others: Developmental and Clinical Aspects of Empathy and Attunement* (pp. 53–76). Lanham, MD: Jason Aronson.

Bernstein, I. & Glenn, J. (1978). The child analyst's emotional reactions to his parents. In: J. Glenn (Ed.), *Child Analysis and Therapy* (pp. 375–392). New York: Jason Aronson.

Bibring, G. L., Dwyer, T. F., Huntington, D. S. & Valenstein, A. F. (1961). A study of the psychological processes in pregnancy and of the earliest mother-child relationship. *Psychoanalytic Study of the Child, 16*: 9–72. New York: International Universities Press.

Bion, W. (1958). On arrogance. *International Journal of Psychoanalysis, 39*: 144–146.

Bion, W. (1962a). *Learning from Experience.* London: Karnac, 1984.

Bion, W. (1962b). A theory of thinking. *International Journal of Psychoanalysis, 43*: 306–310.

Bion, W. (1965). *Transformations.* London: Karnac, 1984.

Bion, W. (1967). Notes on memory and desire. *The Psychoanalytic Forum, 2*: 272–273.

Bion, W. (1970). *Attention and Interpretation.* London: Karnac, 1984.

Blos, P. (1972). Silence: a clinical exploration. *Psychoanalytic Quarterly, 41*: 348–363.

Blum, H. (1987). Countertransference: Concepts and controversies. In: E. Slakter (Ed.), *Countertransference* (pp. 87–104). Northvale, NJ: Jason Aronson.

Blumenthal, R. (2006). Hotel log hints at illicit desire that Dr Freud did not repress. *The New York Times*, p. A-1, December 24.

Boesky, D. (1989). Enactments, acting out, and considerations of reality. Paper presented at the Panel on Enactments, Fall Meeting of the American Psychoanalytic Association, December.

Boesky, D. (1990). The psychoanalytic process and its components. *Psychoanalytic Quarterly*, 59: 550–584.

Bollas, C. (1992). *Being a Character: Psychoanalysis and Self Experience*. New York: Hill & Wang.

Bos, J. & Groenendijk, L. (2006). T*he Self-Marginalization of Wilhelm Stekel: Freudian Circles Inside and Out.* New York: Springer.

Bosteels, B. (2012). *Marx and Freud in Latin America: Politics, Psychoanalysis, and Religion in Times of Terror.* London: Verso.

Boyer, B. (1979). Countertranference with severely regressed patients. In: L. Epstein & A. H. Feiner (Eds.), *Countertransference* (pp. 347–374). New York: Jason Aronson.

Boyer, B. (1980). *Psychoanalytic Treatment of Schizophrenic, Borderline, and Characterological Disorders.* New York: Jason Aronson.

Brakel, L. (1993). Shall drawing become part of free association? *Journal of the American Psychoanalytic Association*, 41: 359–394.

Brenner, C. (1976). *Psychoanalytic Technique and Psychic Conflict.* New York: International Universities Press.

Brenner, C. (2000). Evenly hovering attention. *Psychoanalytic Quarterly*, 69: 545–549.

Breuer, J. & Freud, S. (1895d). Studies on hysteria. *S. E., 2*: 1–17.

Brockbank, R. (1970). On the analyst's silence in psychoanalysis. *International Journal of Psychoanalysis*, 51: 457–464.

Burlingham, D. (1967). Empathy between infant and mother. *Journal of the American Psychoanalytic Association*, 15: 764–780.

Busch, F. (1997). Understanding the patient's use of the method of free association: An ego psychological approach. *Journal of the American Psychoanalytic Association*, 45: 407–423.

Busch, F. (2004). *Ego at the Center of Technique.* Northvale, NJ: Jason Aronson.

Casement, P. (1991). *Learning from the Patient.* New York: Guilford Press.

Cocks, G. (1994). *The Course of Life.* Chicago: University of Chicago Press.

Coen, S. (2002). *Affect Intolerance in Patient and the Analyst.* Northvale, NJ: Jason Aronson.

Coltart, N. (1993). *Slouching Towards Bethlehem.* London: Free Association.

Coltart, N. (1996). Buddhism and psychoanalysis revisited. In: *The Baby and the Bathwater* (pp. 125–139). London: Karnac.

Das, L. S. (1997). *Awakening the Buddha Within*. London: Bantom.

Deutsch, F. (1952). Analytic posturology. *Psychoanalytic Quarterly*, *21*: 196–214.

Dunn, J. (1995). Intersubjectivity in psychoanalysis: A critical review. *International Journal of Psychoanalysis*, *76*: 723–738.

Elson, M. (2001). Silence, its use and abuse: A view from self-psychology. *Clinical Social Work*, *29*: 351–360.

Epstein, M. (1995). Thoughts without a thinker—Buddhism and psychoanalysis. *Psychoanalytic Review*, *92*: 291–406.

Erikson, E. (1958). *Young Man Luther*. New York: W. W. Norton.

Escoll, P. (1999). The "silent" parent and the unprotected, scapegoated child. In: M. R. F. Brescia & M. Lemlij (Eds.), *At the Threshold of the Millennium, Volume 2* (pp. 125–141). Lima, Peru: Sidea/Prom Peru.

Etchegoyen, R. H. (1991). *The Fundamentals of Psychoanalytic Technique*. London, UK: Karnac, 1999.

Feldman, M. (2007). Addressing parts of the self. *International Journal of Psychoanalysis*, *88*: 371–386.

Fenichel, O. (1941). *Problems of Psychoanalytic Technique*. Albany, NY: Psychoanalytic Quarterly Press.

Fenichel, O. (1945). *The Psychoanalytic Theory of Neurosis*. New York: W. W. Norton.

Ferenczi, S. (1911). On obscene words. In: *Contributions to Psycho-Analysis* (pp. 112–130). London: Hogarth, 1948.

Ferenczi, S. (1915). Talkativeness. In: *Further Contributions to the Theory and Technique of Psychoanalysis* (p. 252). London: Hogarth, 1948.

Ferenczi, S. (1916). Silence is golden. In: *Further contributions to the Theory and Technique of Psychoanalysis* (pp. 250–251). London: Hogarth, 1948.

Ferenczi, S. (1929). The unwelcome child and his death instinct. In: *Final Contributions to the Problems and Methods of Psycho-Analysis* (pp. 102–107). London: Hogarth, 1948.

Fivush, R. (2001). Owning experience: The development of subjective perspective in autobiographical memory. In: P. Miller & E. Scholnick (Eds.), *The Self in Time: Developmental Perspectives* (pp. 85–106). New York: Cambridge University Press.

Fivush, R. (2010). Speaking silence: The social construction of silence in autobiographical and cultural narratives. *Memory*, *18*: 88–98.

Fivush, R. & Nelson, K. (2004). Culture and language in the emergence of autobiographical memory. *Psychological Science*, *15*: 586–590.

Fleming, J. & Benedek, T. (1966). *Psychoanalytic Supervision*. New York: Grune & Stratton.

Fliess, R. (1942). The metapsychology of the analyst. *Psychoanalytic Quarterly*, *11*: 211–227.

Fliess, R. (1949). Silence and verbalization: A supplement to the theory of the "analytic rule". *International Journal of Psychoanalysis*, *30*: 21–30.

Fliess, R. (1953). Countertransference and counter-identification. *Journal of the American Psychoanalytic Association*, *1*: 268–281.

Fonagy, P. & Target, M. (1997). Attachment and reflective function: Their role in self-organization. *Development and Psychopathology*, *9*: 679–700.

Fox, R. (1998). The "unobjectionable" countertransference. *Journal of the American Psychoanalytic Association*, *46*: 1067–1087.

Frank, A. (1969). The unrememberable and the unforgettable: Passive primal repression. *Psychoanalytic Study of the Child*, *24*: 48–77.

Freud, A. (1936). *The Ego and the Mechanisms of Defense*. New York: International Universities Press.

Freud, S. (1900a). *The Interpretation of Dreams*. S. E., *4–5*: 1–626.

Freud, S. (1905e). Fragment of an analysis of a case of hysteria. S. E., *7*: 1–122.

Freud, S. (1909d). Notes upon a case of obsessional neurosis. S. E., *10*: 151–318.

Freud, S. (1910d). The future prospects of psycho-analytic therapy. S. E., *11*: 139–152.

Freud, S. (1911e). The handling of dream-interpretation in psycho-analysis. S. E., *12*: 89–96.

Freud, S. (1912b). The dynamics of transference. S. E., *12*: 97–108.

Freud, S. (1912e). Recommendations to physicians practicing psycho-analysis. S. E., *12*: 109–120.

Freud, S. (1913c). On beginning the treatment. S. E., *12*: 123–144.

Freud, S. (1913i). The disposition to obsessional neurosis. S. E., *12*: 311–320.

Freud, S. (1914g). Remembering, repeating, and working-through. S. E., *12*: 145–156.

Freud, S. (1915a). Observations on transference-love. S. E., *12*: 157–171.

Freud, S. (1917). General theory of the neuroses. S. E., *16*: 243–256.

Freud, S. (1917). Introductory lectures on psycho-analysis, XXIII. S. E., *16*: 358–377.

Freud, S. (1930a). Civilization and its discontents. S. E., *21*: 59–145.

Freud, S. (1931b). Female sexuality. S. E., *21*: 221–243.

Freud, S. (1937c). Analysis terminable and interminable. S. E., *23*: 211–253.

Freud, S. (1940a). An outline of psycho-analysis. S. E., *23*: 139–207.

Fromm-Reichman, F. (1950). *Principles of Intensive Psychotherapy*. Chicago: University of Chicago Press.

Frosh, S. (1999). *The Politics of Psychoanalysis: An Introduction to Freudian and Post-Freudian Theory* (Second edition). New York: New York University Press.

Gammill, J. (1980). Some reflections on analytic listening and the dream screen. *International Journal of Psychoanalysis, 61*: 357–381.

Gedo, J. E. & Goldberg, A. (1973). *Models of the Mind*. Chicago: University of Chicago Press.

Gill, M. (1979). The analysis of the transference. *Journal of the American Psychoanalytic Association, 27*(Suppl.): 263–288.

Gill, M. (1994). *Psychoanalysis in Transition: A Personal View*. Hillsdale, NJ: Analytic Press.

Giovacchini, P. (2000). *Impact of Narcissism: The Errant Therapist in a Chaotic Quest*. Northvale, NJ: Jason Aronson.

Gitelson, M. (1952). The emotional position of the analyst in the psychoanalytic situation. *International Journal of Psychoanalysis, 33*: 1–10.

Glover, E. (1955). *The Technique of Psychoanalysis*. New York: International Universities Press.

Goldberg, A. (1987). The place of apology in psychoanalysis and psychotherapy. *International Review of Psycho-Analysis, 14*: 409–422.

Gorkin, M. (1996). Countertransference in cross-cultural psychotherapy. In: R. Perez-Foster, M. Moskowitz & R. A. Javier (Eds.), *Reaching across Boundaries of Culture and Class* (pp. 47–70). Northvale, NJ: Jason Aronson.

Gray, P. (1982). Developmental lag in the evolution of technique for psychoanalysis of neurotic conflict. *Journal of the American Psychoanalytic Association, 30*: 621–655.

Gray, P. (1994). *The Ego and the Analysis of Defense*. Northvale, NJ: Jason Aronson.

Green, A. (1983). *Narcissisme de vie, Narcissisme de mort*. Paris: Minuit.

Green, A. (1993). *The Work of the Negative*. London: Free Association.

Greenson, R. (1960). Empathy and its vicissitudes. *International Journal of Psychoanalysis, 41*: 418–424.

Greenson, R. (1961). On the silence and sounds of the analytic hour. *Journal of the American Psychoanalytic Association, 9*: 79–84.

Greenson, R. (1965). The working alliance and the transference neurosis. *Psychoanalytic Quarterly, 34*: 155–181.

Greenson, R. (1967). *The Technique and Practice of Psychoanalysis*. New York: International Universities Press.

Grenville, K. (2007). Unsettling the settler: history, culture, race, and the Australian self. In: M. T. S. Hooke & S. Akhtar (Eds.), *The Geography of Meanings: Psychoanalytic Perspectives on Place, Space, Land, and Dislocation* (pp. 49–62). London: International Psychoanalytical Association.

Griefinger, J. (1997). On the horizon of authenticity: Toward a moral account of psychoanalytic therapy. In: C. Spezzano & G. J. Gargiulo (Eds.),

Soul on the Couch: Spirituality, Religion, and Morality in Contemporary Psychoanalysis (pp. 201–230). Hillsdale, NJ: Analytic Press.

Grinberg, L. & Grinberg, R. (1989). *Psychoanalytic Perspectives on Migration and Exile*. New Haven, CT: Yale University Press.

Grotjahn, M. (1955). Problems and techniques of supervision. *Psychiatry, 18*: 9–15.

Guntrip, H. (1969). *Schizoid Phenomena, Object Relations and the Self*. New York: International Universities Press.

Guntrip, H. (1975). My experience of analysis with Fairbairn and Winnicott. *International Review of Psycho-Analysis, 2*: 145–156.

Haesler, L. (1993). Adequate distance in the relationship between supervisor and supervisee. *International Journal of Psychoanalysis, 74*: 547–555.

Hedges, L. E. (1983). *Listening Perspectives in Psychotherapy*. Northvale, NJ: Jason Aronson.

Heimann, P. (1950). On countertransference. *International Journal of Psychoanalysis, 31*: 81–84.

Herzog, J. (1984). Fathers and young children: Fathering daughters and fathering sons. In: J. D. Call, E. Galenson & R. Tyson (Eds.), *Foundations of Infant Psychiatry, Vol 2* (pp. 335–343). New York: Basic.

Hinshelwood, R. (1989). *A Dictionary of Kleinian Thought*. Northvale, NJ: Jason Aronson.

Hirsch, I. (1998). The concept of enactment and theoretical convergence. *Psychoanalytic Quarterly, 67*: 78–100.

Hoffer, W. (1956). Transference and transference neurosis. *International Journal of Psychoanalysis, 37*: 377–379.

Hoffer, A. (2006). What does the analyst want: Free association in relation to the analyst's activity, ambition, and technical innovation. *American Journal of Psychoanalysis, 66*: 1–23.

Hoffman, I. Z. (1991). Discussion: towards a social-constructivist view of the psychoanalytic situation. *Psychoanalytic Dialogues, 1*: 74–105.

Hollander, N. C. (2010). *Uprooted Minds: Surviving the Politics of Terror in the Americas*. New York: Routledge.

Hopkins, L. (2006). *False Self: The Life of Masud Khan*. New York: Other Press.

Hora, T. (1957). Contribution to the phenomenology of the supervisory process. *American Journal of Psychotherapy, 11*: 769–773.

Horowitz, M. (1975). Sliding meanings: A defense against threat in narcissistic personalities. *International Journal of Psychoanalytic Psychotherapy, 4*: 167–180.

Isaacs, S. (1939). Criteria for interpretation. *International Journal of Psychoanalysis, 20*: 148–160.

Isakower, O. (1963a). Minutes of New York Psychoanalytic Institute faculty meeting, October 14, unpublished.

Isakower, O. (1963b). Minutes of New York Psychoanalytic Institute faculty meeting, November 20, unpublished.

Ivey, G. (2008). Enactment controversies: A critical review of current debates. *International Journal of Psychoanalysis, 88*: 19–38.

Jacobs, M. (2011). Interpreting in the form of action. In: S. Akhtar (Ed.), *Unusual Interventions: Alterations of the Frame Method, and Relationship in Psychotherapy and Psychoanalysis* (pp. 113–137). London: Karnac.

Jacobs, T. J. (1973). Posture, gesture, and movement in the analyst: Cues to interpretation and countertransference. *Journal of the American Psychoanalytic Association, 21*: 77–92.

Jacobs, T. J. (1983). The analyst and the patient's object world: Notes on an aspect of countertransference. *Journal of the American Psychoanalytic Association, 31*: 619–642.

Jacobs, T. J. (1986). On countertransference enactments. *Journal of the American Psychoanalytic Association, 34*: 289–307.

Jacobs, T. J. (1991). *The Use of the Self: Countertransference and Communication in the Analytic Situation.* Madison, CT: International Universities Press.

Jacobs, T. J. (1992). Isakower's ideas of the analytic instrument and contemporary views of analytic listening. *Journal of Clinical Psychoanalysis, 1*: 237–241.

Jacobs, T. J. (2007). Listening, dreaming, sharing: On the uses of the analyst's inner experiences. In: S. Akhtar (Ed.), *Listening to Others: Developmental and Clinical Aspects of Empathy and Attunement* (pp. 93–112). Lanham, MD: Jason Aronson.

Joseph, B. (1987). Projective identification: some clinical aspects. In: E. B. Spillius (Ed.), *Melanie Klein Today, I: Mainly Theory* (pp. 138–150). London: Routledge, 1988.

Kafka, J. (1989). *Multiple Realities in Clinical Practice.* New Haven, CT: Yale University Press.

Kanzer, M. (1958). Image formation during free association. *Psychoanalytic Quarterly, 27*: 465–484.

Katan, A. (1961). Some thoughts about the role of verbalization in early childhood. *Psychoanalytic Study of the Child, 16*: 184–198.

Kernberg, O. F. (1975). *Borderline Conditions and Pathological Narcissism.* New York: Jason Aronson.

Kernberg, O. F. (1984). *Severe Personality Disorders: Psychotherapeutic Strategies.* New Haven, CT: Yale University Press.

Kernberg, O. F. (1992). *Aggression in Personality Disorders and Perversions.* New Haven, CT: Yale University Press.

Kernberg, O. F., Selzer, M. A., Koenigsberg, H. W., Carr, A. C. & Appelbaum, A. H. (1989). *Psychodynamic Psychotherapy of Borderline Patients*. New York: Basic.

Khan, M. (1983a). On lying fallow. In: *Hidden Selves: Between Theory and Practice in Psychoanalysis* (pp. 183–188). New York: International Universities Press.

Khan, M. (1983b). Infancy, aloneness and madness. In: *Hidden Selves: Between Theory and Practice in Psychoanalysis* (pp. 181–182). New York: International Universities Press.

Killingmo, B. (1989). Conflict and deficit: Implications for technique. *International Journal of Psychoanalysis, 70*: 65–79.

Klauber, J. (1968). The psychoanalyst as a person. In: *Difficulties in the Analytic Encounter* (pp. 123–139). New York: Jason Aronson, 1976.

Klein, M. (1926). The psychological principles of early analysis. *International Journal of Psychoanalysis, 7*: 31–63.

Klein, M. (1935). A contribution to the psychogenesis of manic depressive states. In: *Love, Guilt and Reparation and Other Works 1921–1945* (pp. 262–289). New York: Free Press, 1975.

Klein, M. (1940). Mourning and its relation to manic depressive states. In: *Love, Guilt and Reparation and Other Works—1921–1945* (pp. 344–369). New York: Free Press, 1975.

Klein, M. (1946). Notes on some schizoid mechanisms. In: J. Mitchell (Ed.), *The Selected Melanie Klein* (pp. 175–200). New York: Free Press, 1986.

Klein, M. (1952). The mutual influences in the development of ego and the id. In: *Envy and Gratitude and Other Works 1946–1963* (pp. 57–60). New York: Free Press, 1975.

Klein, M. (1955). The psychoanalytic play technique: Its history and significance. In: *Envy and Gratitude and Other Works 1946–1963* (pp. 122–140). New York: Free Press, 1975.

Kohut, H. (1971). *Analysis of the Self*. New York: International Universities Press.

Kohut, H. (1977). *The Restoration of the Self*. New York: International Universities Press.

Kohut, H. (1979). Two analyses of Mr Z. *International Journal of Psychoanalysis, 60*: 3–27.

Kohut, H. (1980). Summarizing reflections. In: A. Goldberg (Ed.), *Advances in Self Psychology* (pp. 473–554). New York: International Universities Press.

Kohut, H. (1982). Introspection, empathy, and the semi-circle of mental health. *International Journal of Psychoanalysis, 63*: 395–407.

Kohut, H. (1984). *How Does Analysis Cure?* Chicago: University of Chicago Press.

Kolvin, I. & Fundudis, T. (1981). Electively mute children: Psychological development and background factors. *Journal of Child Psychiatry*, 22: 219–232.

Kramer, S. & Akhtar, S. (1988). The developmental content of internalized preoedipal object relations. *Psychoanalytic Quarterly*, 42: 547–576.

Kreuzer-Haustein, U. (1994). On the analyst's silence. *Forum der Psychoanalyse: Zeitschrift für klinische Theorie und Praxis*, 10: 21–42.

Kris, A. O. (1982). *Free Association*. New Haven, CT: Yale University Press.

Kris, A. O. (1992). Interpretation and the method of free association. *Psychoanalytic Inquiry*, 12: 208–224.

Kristeva, J. (1988). *Étrangers à nous mêmes*. Paris: Fayard.

Layton, L., Hollander, N. C. & Gutwill, S. (2006). *Psychoanalysis, Class and Politics: Encounters in the Clinical Setting*. New York: Routledge.

Levenson, E. A. (1982). Follow the fox—an inquiry into the vicissitudes of psychoanalytic supervision. *Contemporary Psychoanalysis*, 18: 1–15.

Levy, J. (1995). Analytic stalemate and supervision. *Psychoanalytic Inquiry*, 15: 169–189.

Lhulier, J. (2005). Learning in an increasingly multitheoretical psychoanalytic culture: Impact on the development of psychoanalytic identity. *Psychoanalytic Psychology*, 22: 459–472.

Little, M. (1951). Countertransference and the patient's response to it. *International Journal of Psychoanalysis*, 32: 32–40.

Little, M. (1960). Countertransference. *British Journal of Medical Psychology*, 33: 29–31.

Loewald, H. (1960). On the therapeutic action of psychoanalysis. *Journal of the American Psychoanalytic Association*, 41: 16–33.

Loewenstein, R. (1951). The problem of interpretation. *Psychoanalytic Quarterly*, 20: 1–23.

Loewenstein, R. (1956). Some remarks on the role of speech in psychoanalytic technique. *International Journal of Psychoanalysis* 35: 188–211.

Loewenstein, R. (1961). The silent patient: Introduction. *Journal of the American Psychoanalytic Association*, 9: 2–6.

Loomie, L. (1961). Some ego considerations in the silent patient. *Journal of the American Psychoanalytic Association*, 9: 56–78.

Maeder, T. (1989). *Children of Psychiatrists and Other Psychotherapists*. New York: Harper & Row.

Mahler, M. S., Pine, F. & Bergman, A. (1975). *The Psychological Birth of the Human Infant: Symbiosis and Individuation*. New York: Basic.

Makari, G.. & Shapiro, T. (1993). On psychoanalytic listening: Language and unconscious communication. *Journal of the American Psychoanalytic Association*, 41: 991–102.

McDermott, V. (2003). Panel report: Is free association still fundamental? *Journal of the American Psychoanalytic Association*, 51: 1349–1356.

McDougall, J. (1985). *Theaters of the Mind: Illusion and Truth on the Psychoanalytic Stage*. New York: Brunner/Mazel.

McLaughlin, J. (1987). The play of transference: Some reflections on enactment in the psychoanalytic situation. *Journal of the American Psychoanalytic Association*, 35: 557–582.

McLaughlin, J. (1992). Non-verbal behaviors in the analytic situation: The search for meaning in non-verbal cues. In: S. Kramer & S. Akhtar (Eds.), *When the Body Speaks: Psychological Meanings in Kinetic Clues* (pp. 131–161). Northvale, NJ: Jason Aronson.

Meissner, W. (1984). *Psychoanalysis and Religious Experience*. New Haven, CT: Yale University Press.

Meissner, W. (2000). On analytic listening. *Psychoanalytic Quarterly*, 69: 317–368.

Meissner, W. (2001). So help me God!: Do I help God or does God help me? In: S. Akhtar & H. Parens (Eds.), *Does God Help? Developmental and Clinical Aspects of Religious Belief* (pp. 74–126). Northvale, NJ: Jason Aronson.

Miller, P. & Aisentein, M. (2004). Panel report: On analytic listening. *International Journal of Psychoanalysis*, 85: 1485–1488.

Mitchell, S. A. (1988). *Relational Concepts in Psychoanalysis*. Boston, MA: Harvard University Press.

Mitchell, S. A. (1991). Wishes, needs, and interpersonal negotiations. *Psychoanalytic Inquiry*, 11: 147–170.

Mitchell, S. A. (1993). *Hope and Dread in Psychoanalysis*. New York: Basic.

Mitchell, S. A. & Aron, L. (1999). *Relational Psychoanalysis: The Emergence of a Tradition*. Hillsdale, NJ: Analytic Press.

Mitrani, J. (2001). *Ordinary People and Extraordinary Protections*. London: Brunner-Routledge.

Modell, A. (1975). A narcissistic defense against affect and the illusion of self sufficiency. *International Journal of Psychoanalysis*, 56: 275–282.

Money-Kyrle, R. (1956). Normal countertransference and some of its deviations. *International Journal of Psychoanalysis*, 37: 360–366.

Moore, B. & Fine, B. (1995). *Psychoanalysis: The Major Concepts*. New Haven, CT: Yale University Press.

Nacht, S. (1964). Silence as an integrative factor. *International Journal of Psychoanalysis*, 45: 299–303.

Nersessian, E. & Kopf, R. (1996). *Textbook of Psychoanalysis*. Washington, DC: American Psychiatric Press.

Nichol, D. (2006). Buddhism and psychoanalysis: A personal reflection. *American Journal of Psychoanalysis*, 66: 157–172.

Nichols, M. (2009). *The Lost Art of Listening: How Learning to Listen Can Improve Relationships*. New York: Guilford Press.

Nosek, L. (2009). Body and infinite: Notes for a theory of genitality. *International Journal of Psychoanalysis, 90: Revista Brasiliera de Psicanalise* 43: 139–151.

Ogden, T. H. (1986). *The Matrix of the Mind: Object Relations and the Psycho-analytic Dialogue*. Northvale, NJ: Jason Aronson.

Ogden, T. H. (1992). The dialectically constituted/decentered subject of psychoanalysis. *International Journal of Psychoanalysis, 73*: 517–526.

Ogden, T. H. (1994). *Subjects of Analysis*. Northvale, NJ: Jason Aronson.

Olinick, S. (1969). On empathy and regression in the service of the other. *British Journal of Medical Psychology, 42*: 41–49.

Olinick, S., Poland, W., Grigg, K. & Granatir, W. (1973). The psycho-analytic work ego: Process and interpretation. *International Journal of Psychoanalysis, 54*: 143–151.

Ostow, M. (2001). Three archaic contributions to the religious instinct: awe, mysticism, and apocalypse. In: S. Akhtar & H. Parens (Eds.), *Does God Help? Developmental and Clinical Aspects of Religious Belief* (pp. 197–233). Northvale, NJ: Jason Aronson.

Paniagua, C. (1998). Acting-in revisited. *International Journal of Psychoanalysis, 79*: 449–512.

Paniagua, C. (2004). What has happened to the body in psychoanalysis. *International Journal of Psychoanalysis, 85*: 973–976.

Parsons, M. (2007). Raiding the inarticulate: The internal analytic setting and listening beyond countertransference. *International Journal of Psychoanalysis, 88*: 1441–1456.

Pegeron, J. (1996). Supervision as an analytic experience. *Psychoanalytic Quarterly, 65*: 693–710.

Person, E., Cooper, A. & Gabbard, G. (2005). *Textbook of Psychoanalysis*. Washington, DC: American Psychiatric Press.

Pine, F. (1988). The four psychologies of psychoanalysis and their place in clinical work. *Journal of the American Psychoanalytic Association, 36*: 571–596.

Pine, F. (1997). *Diversity and Direction in Psychoanalytic Technique*. New Haven, CT: Yale University Press.

Poland, W. (1975). Tact as a psychoanalytic function. *International Journal of Psychoanalysis, 56*: 155–161.

Poland, W. (1996). *Melting the Darkness: The Dyad and Principles of Clinical Practice*. Northvale, NJ: Jason Aronson.

Prathikanti, S. (1997). East Indian American families. In: E. Lee (Ed.), *Working with Asian Americans: A Guide to Clinicians* (pp.79–100). New York: Guilford Press.

Pulver, S. (1992). Gestures, emblems, and body language: What does it all mean? In: S. Kramer & S. Akhtar (Eds.), *When the Body Speaks: Psychological Meanings in Kinetic Clues* (pp. 163–177). Northvale, NJ: Jason Aronson.

Racker, H. (1953). A contribution to the problem of countertransference. *International Journal of Psychoanalysis, 34*: 313–324.

Racker, H. (1957). The meanings and uses of countertransference. *Psychoanalytic Quarterly, 26*: 303–357.

Racker, H. (1958). Psychoanalytic technique and the analyst's unconscious masochism. *Psychoanalytic Quarterly, 37*: 555–562.

Racker, H. (1968). *Transference and Countertransference*. New York: International Universities Press.

Reich, A. (1951). On countertransference. *International Journal of Psychoanalysis, 32*: 25–31.

Reich, W. (1933). *Character Analysis*. New York: Farrar, Straus and Giroux, 1972.

Reik, T. (1937). *Surprise and the Psychoanalyst*. New York: Dutton.

Reik, T. (1948). *Listening with the Third Ear*. New York: Farrar, Straus and Giroux, 1983.

Reik, T. (1968). The psychological meaning of silence. *Psychoanalytic Review, 55*: 176–186.

Renik, O. (1993). Analytic interaction: Conceptualizing technique in light of the analyst's irreducible subjectivity. *Psychoanalytic Quarterly, 62*: 553–571.

Riess, A. (1978). The mother's eye: For better and for worse. *Psychoanalytic Study of the Child, 33*: 381–433.

Rilton, A. (1988). Some thoughts on supervision. *Scandinavian Psychoanalytic Review, 11*: 106–116.

Riviere, J. (1952). General introduction. In: E. Jones (Ed.), *Developments in Psycho-Analysis*, (pp. 1–36). London: Hogarth.

Rizzuto, A. M. (1979). *The Birth of the Living God*. Chicago: University of Chicago Press.

Rizzuto, A. M. (1996). Psychoanalytic treatment and the religious person. In: E. Sahfranske (Ed.), *Religion and Clinical Practice of Psychology* (pp. 409–432). Washington, DC: American Psychological Association.

Rizzuto, A. M. (2001). Does God help? What God? Helping whom? The convolutions of divine help. In: S. Akhtar & H. Parens (Eds.), *Does God Help? Developmental and Clinical Aspects of Religious Belief* (pp. 19–52). Northvale, NJ: Jason Aronson.

Roberts, S. J. (2002). Identifying mutism's etiology in a child. *The Nurse Practitioner, 27*: 44–48.

Roland, A. (1996). *Cultural Pluralism and Psychoanalysis: The Asian and North American Experience*. New York: Routledge.

Ronningstam, E. (2006). Silence: Cultural function and psychological transformation in psychoanalysis and psychoanalytic psychotherapy. *International Journal of Psychoanalysis, 87*: 1277–1295.

Rosen, B. (2000). Through the looking glass (darkly): The "training neurosis" and the development of an analytic identity. *Journal of Clinical Psychoanalysis, 9*: 39–50.

Rubin, J. (1996). *Psychotherapy and Buddhism: Toward an Integration*. New York: Plenum Press.

Sabbadini, A. (1992). Listening to silence. *Scandinavian Psychoanalytic Review, 15*: 27–36.

San Roque, C. (2007). Coming to terms with the country: some incidents on first meeting Aboriginal locations and Aboriginal thoughts. In: M. T. S. Hooke & S. Akhtar (Eds.), *The Geography of Meanings: Psychoanalytic Perspectives on Place, Space, Land, and Dislocation* (pp. 105–140). London: International Psychoanalytical Association.

Sander, L. (1975). Infant and caretaking environment: Investigation and conceptualization of adaptive behavior in a system of increasing complexity. In: E. J. Anthony (Ed.), *Explorations in Child Psychiatry* (pp. 129–166). New York: Plenum Press.

Sandler, J. (1960). The background of safety. *International Journal of Psychoanalysis, 41*: 352–365.

Sandler, J. (1976). Countertransference and role responsiveness. *International Review of Psycho-Analysis, 3*: 43–47.

Sandler, J., Dare, C. & Holder, A. (1973). *The Patient and the Analyst*. New York: International Universities Press.

Sandler, J. & Sandler, A. M. (1998). *Internal Objects Revisited*. London: Karnac.

Sartre, J. -P. (1946). *No Exit and Three Other Plays*. New York: Vintage.

Schafer, R. (1976). *A New Language for Psychoanalysis*. New Haven, CT: Yale University Press.

Schafer, R. (1978). *Language and Insight*. Northvale, NJ: Jason Aronson.

Schlesinger, H. (2003). *The Texture of Treatment: On the Matter of Psychoanalytic Technique*. Hillsdale, NJ: Analytic Press.

Schwaber, E. A. (1981). Empathy: A mode of analytic listening. *Psychoanalytic Inquiry, 1*: 357–392.

Schwaber, E. A. (1983). Psychoanalytic listening and psychic reality. *International Review of Psycho-Analysis, 10*: 378–392.

Schwaber, E. A. (1995). The psychoanalyst's mind: From listening to interpretation: A clinical report. *International Journal of Psychoanalysis, 76*: 271–281.

Schwaber, E. A. (1998). The non-verbal dimension in psychoanalysis. *International Journal of Psychoanalysis, 79*: 667–689.

Schwaber, E. A. (2005). The struggle to listen: Continuing reflections, lingering paradoxes, and some thoughts on recovery of memory. *Journal of the American Psychoanalytic Association, 53*: 789–810.

Schwaber, E. A. (2007). The unending struggle to listen: Locating oneself within the other. In: S. Akhtar (Ed.), *Listening to Others: Developmental and Clinical Aspects of Empathy and Attunement* (pp. 17–39). Lanham, MD: Jason Aronson.

Searles, H. F. (1955). The informational value of the supervisor's emotional experience. *Psychiatry, 18*: 135–146.

Searles, H. F. (1979). The analyst's experience with jealousy. In: L. Epstein & A. Feiner (Eds.), *Countertransference* (pp. 305–327). New York: Jason Aronson.

Shafii, M. (1973). Silence in the service of ego: Psychoanalytic study of meditation. *International Journal of Psychoanalysis, 54*: 431–443.

Shapiro, E. & Pinsker, H. (1973). Shared ethnic scotoma. *American Journal of Psychiatry, 130*: 1338–1341.

Shapiro, T. (1979). *Clinical Psycholinguistics*. New York: Plenum Press.

Sharpe, E. F. (1940). Psychophysical problems revealed in language: an examination of metaphor. In: *Collected Papers on Psychoanalysis* (pp. 155–169). London: Hogarth, 1950.

Sharpe, E. F. (1947). The psychoanalyst. *International Journal of Psychoanalysis, 28*: 1–6.

Shengold, L. (1989). *Soul Murder: The Effects of Childhood Abuse and Deprivation*. New Haven, CT: Yale University Press.

Siegman, A. (1954). Emotionality: a hysterical character defense. *Psychoanalytic Quarterly, 23*: 339–354.

Silberer, H. (1914). *Problem der Mystik und ihrer Symbolik*. Leipzig, Germany: Hugo Heller.

Skolnikoff, A. Z. (2000). Seeking an analytic identity. *Psychoanalytic Inquiry, 20*: 594–610.

Slakter, E. (1987). *Countertransference*. Northvale, NJ: Jason Aronson.

Slap, J. W. (1976). A note on the drawing of dream details. *Psychoanalytic Quarterly, 45*: 455–456.

Smith, H. F. (1999). Subjectivity and objectivity in analytic listening. *Journal of the American Psychoanalytic Association, 47*: 465–484.

Smolar, A. (2002). Reflections on gifts in the therapeutic setting: The gift from patient to therapist. *American Journal of Psychotherapy, 56*: 27–45.

Solnit, A. J. (1970). Learning from psychoanalytic supervision. *International Journal of Psychoanalysis, 51*: 359–362.

Sonnenberg, S. M. (1995). Analytic listening and the analyst's self-analysis. *International Journal of Psychoanalysis*, *76*: 335–342.

Spencer, J. H. & Balter, L. (1990). Psychoanalytic observation. *Journal of the American Psychoanalytic Association*, *38*: 393–421.

Spezzano, C. (1993). *Affects in Psychoanalysis: A Clinical Synthesis*. Hillsdale, NJ: Analytic Press.

Spivak, G. C. (1988). Can the subaltern speak? In: C. Nelson & L. Grossberg (Eds.), *Marxism and the Interpretation of Culture* (pp. 283–298). Champagne-Urbana, IL: University of Illinois Press.

Steel, E. (2007). Lost children. In: M. T. S. Hooke & S. Akhtar (Eds.), *The Geography of Meanings: Psychoanalytic Perspectives on Place, Space, Land, and Dislocation* (pp. 79–104). London: International Psychoanalytical Association.

Stolorow, R. & Atwood, G. (1978). *Faces in a Cloud: Subjectivity in Personality Theory*. New York: Jason Aronson.

Stolorow, R. D., Brandchaft, B. & Atwood, G. E. (1987). *Psychoanalytic Treatment: An Intersubjective Approach*. Hillsdale, NJ: Analytic Press.

Stolorow, R. D., Brandchaft, B. & Atwood, G. E. (1992). *Context of Being: The Intersubjectivist Foundations of Psychological Life*. Hillsdale, NJ: Analytic Press.

Stone, L. (1961). *The Psychoanalytic Situation*. New York: International Universities Press.

Stone, M. (2009). Lying and deceitfulness in personality disorders. In: S. Akhtar (Ed.), *Lying, Cheating, and Carrying On* (pp. 69–92). Lanham, MD: Jason Aronson.

Strenger, C. (1989). The classic and the romantic visions in psychoanalysis. *International Journal of Psychoanalysis*, *70*: 595–610.

Strozier, C. (2004). *Heinz Kohut: the Making of a Psychoanalyst*. New York: Other Press.

Sullivan, H. S. (1947). *Conceptions of Modern Psychiatry*. Washington, DC: William Alanson White Foundation.

Sullivan, H. S. (1953). *The Interpersonal Theory of Psychiatry*. New York: W. W. Norton.

Suslick, A. (1969). Nonverbal communication in the analysis of adults. *Journal of the American Psychoanalytic Association*, *17*: 955–967.

Tang, N. M. & Gardner, J. (1999). Race, culture, and psychotherapy: Transference to minority therapists. *Psychoanalytic Quarterly*, *68*: 1–20.

Target, M. & Fonagy, P. (1996). Playing with reality II: The development of psychic reality from a theoretical perspective. *International Journal of Psychoanalysis*, *77*: 459–479.

Thedailybeast.com/articles/2011/12/20/rick-perry-s-kim-jong-il-slip-oops-moment-and-more-gaffes.html

Thomson, J. A. (2001). Does God help me or do I help God or neither? In: S. Akhtar & H. Parens (Eds.), *Does God Help?: Developmental and Clinical Aspects of Religious Belief* (pp. 127–152). Northvale, NJ: Jason Aronson.

Van der Heide, C. (1961). Blank silence and the dream screen. *Journal of the American Psychoanalytic Association, 9*: 85–90.

Volkan, V. D. (1976). *Primitive Internalized Object Relations.* New York: International Universities Press.

Volkan, V. D. (1987). *Six Steps in the Treatment of Borderline Personality Organization.* Northvale, NJ: Jason Aronson.

Volkan, V. D. (2010). *Psychoanalytic Technique Expanded: A Textbook on Psychoanalytic Treatment.* Istanbul, Turkey: OA Books.

Waelder, R. (1936). The principle of multiple function: Observations on multiple determination. *Psychoanalytic Quarterly, 41*: 283–290.

Wantuch, E. (2002). Adult onset hearing loss and its impact on the psychotherapist-client relationship. *Dissertation Abstracts, 62*: 4241.

Warren, M. (1961). The significance of visual images during the analytic session. *Journal of the American Psychoanalytic Association, 9*: 504–518.

Winnicott, D. W. (1935). The manic defense. In: *Through Paediatrics to Psychoanalysis: Collected Papers* (pp. 129–144). New York: Brunner/Mazel, 1992.

Winnicott, D. W. (1947). Hate in the countertransference. In: *Collected Papers: Through Paediatrics to Psychoanalysis* (pp. 306–316). New York: Basic, 1958.

Winnicott, D. W. (1953). Transitional objects and transitional phenomena: a study of the first not- me object. *International Journal of Psychoanalysis, 34*: 89–97.

Winnicott, D. W. (1956). Primary maternal preoccupation. In: *Collected Papers: Through Paediatrics to Psychoanalysis* (pp. 300–305). New York: Basic, 1958.

Winnicott, D. W. (1960a). Ego distortion in terms of true and false self. In: *The Maturational Processes and the Facilitating Environment* (pp. 140–152). New York: International Universities Press, 1965.

Winnicott, D. W. (1960b). Countertransference. *British Journal of Medical Psychology, 33*: 17–21.

Winnicott, D. W. (1963). Communicating and not communicating leading to a study of certain opposites. In: *The Maturational Processes and the Facilitating Environment* (pp. 166–170). New York: International Universities Press, 1965.

Winnicott, D. W. (1965). *Maturational Environment and Facilitating Processes.* New York: International Universities Press.

Winnicott, D. W. (1966). Ordinary devoted mother. In: C. Winnicott, R. Shepherd & M. Davis (Eds.), *Babies and Their Mothers* (pp. 3–4). Reading, MA: Addison-Wiley, 1987.

Wolf, E. (1979). Countertransference in disorders of the self. In: L. Epstein & A. H. Feiner (Eds.), *Countertransference: The Therapist's Contribution to the Therapeutic Situation* (pp. 445–464). New York: Jason Aronson.

Wong P. (2010). Selective mutism: a review of etiology, comorbidities, and treatment. *Psychiatry, 7*: 23–31.

Wright, K. (1991). *Vision and Separation between Mother and Baby.* Northvale, NJ: Jason Aronson.

Wurmser, L. (2000). Magic transformation and tragic transformation: Splitting of the ego and superego in severely traumatized patients. *Clinical Social Work, 28*: 385–395.

Zeligs, M. A. (1957). Acting in: A contribution to the meaning of some postural attitudes observed during analysis. *Journal of the American Psychoanalytic Association, 5*: 685–706.

Zeligs, M. A. (1960). The role of silence in transference, countertransference and the psychoanalytic process. *International Journal of Psychoanalysis, 41*: 407–412.

Zeligs, M. A. (1961). The psychology of silence: Its role in transference, countertransference, and the psychoanalytic process. *Journal of the American Psychoanalytic Association, 9*: 7–43.

Zetzel, E. (1956). Current concepts of transference. *International Journal of Psychoanalysis, 37*: 369–375.

INDEX